THE SMART NEANDERTHAL

THE SMART
NEANDERTHAL

bird catching, cave art & the cognitive revolution

CLIVE FINLAYSON

OXFORD
UNIVERSITY PRESS

OXFORD
UNIVERSITY PRESS

Great Clarendon Street, Oxford, OX2 6DP,
United Kingdom

Oxford University Press is a department of the University of Oxford.
It furthers the University's objective of excellence in research, scholarship,
and education by publishing worldwide. Oxford is a registered trade mark of
Oxford University Press in the UK and in certain other countries

© Clive Finlayson 2019

The moral rights of the author have been asserted

First Edition published in 2019
Impression: 1

Published in the United States of America by Oxford University Press
198 Madison Avenue, New York, NY 10016, United States of America

British Library Cataloguing in Publication Data
Data available

Library of Congress Control Number: 2018942779

ISBN 978-0-19-879752-4

Printed and bound by
Clays Ltd, Elcograf S.p.A.

To Geraldine and Stewart
Fellow Travellers in this Journey of Discovery

CONTENTS

CONTENTS

CONTENTS

PREFACE

This book combines my two scientific passions: the study of birds and of Neanderthals. Birds came first, from my childhood, and I have my late father to thank for exposing me to that particular world which had been his own passion. It was through birds that I entered the fields of biogeography and evolutionary ecology which are my main areas of research. I must have been very young when I started; I cannot be certain when, but I wrote down my first observations when I was eleven so it must have been quite some time before that.

Although my formal interest in Neanderthals started in 1989 when Chris Stringer and Andy Currant of the Natural History Museum in London came to Gibraltar in search of Neanderthals, my deep interest in the discoveries made by the Leakeys in East Africa go back to my schooldays. The two passions conspired to bring me to where I am today.

I took Chris and Andy to Gorham's Cave, because it was a place that I knew well from my study of the crag martins which roosted in there each winter. I recall being with Geraldine, whom I would later marry, in these caves, catching the birds for study and discussing who might have lived in these spectacular caverns and what they might have been like. We knew at the time that some archaeological work had been done here in the 1950s and that Neanderthals had occupied the cave, but that was about it.

After all these years of working in these caves, coming up to thirty years for Geraldine and me, birds and Neanderthals inevitably came together. Who would have thought when we started that we would find direct evidence of Neanderthal exploitation of birds, not just for food but also so as to wear their feathers? The birds told us much more than this. Geraldine devoted her PhD thesis to describing the landscape of the Neanderthals in great detail, thanks to the information provided by birds.

Our son Stewart first went down to the caves when he was eight. He spent big chunks of his childhood with us in the Doñana National Park in south-western Spain, as Geraldine took detailed notes of birds and their habitats for her research. He learnt his trade here and, through me, was captivated by his grandfather's passion for birds. He is now working with Neanderthals and birds for his own PhD thesis, looking at how Neanderthals interacted with birds and what birds can tell us about Neanderthal ecology and responses to climate. In reality, this book could not have been written without Geraldine's and Stewart's massive contribution. They are the two silent co-authors.

Although many have contributed to the work in the caves, there are five people who have been fundamental to the story that I will tell in this book. They are Ruth Blasco, Gary Bortolotti, Juan Jose Negro, Antonio Sanchez Marco, and Jordi Rosell. I will introduce them at different points in the book.

This book tells the story of how we discovered the relationship which Neanderthals had with birds. The story is not yet complete, but we have enough to be able to tell it as we understand it today. Stewart's work is going to provide us with further glimpses into the world of the Neanderthals and I am sure that others will follow. This connection between Neanderthals and birds is not trivial. It talks to us of Neanderthal abilities and capacities. Those who have sought to define what modern human behaviour is, always relegating the Neanderthals to an archaic world of primitiveness in the process, now have to revisit their untenable position.

We are at the most important interface in the understanding of human origins and evolution since studies began. With the powerful tool provided by the study of ancient DNA we are finding that the Neanderthal–Modern Human boundary, so clear-cut when we started our work, has broken down. We are finding other human lineages, like the Denisovans, discovered from small fragments of bone so insignificant that we would never have been able to recognize their distinctiveness from anatomy alone. We are redefining the Neanderthals and, in the process, finding out who we are and where we came from. It isn't the simple Out-of-Africa narrative that we grew up with, and there was no simple 'Cognitive Revolution'. In this journey of rediscovery it has become abundantly clear that, ironically, the Neanderthals had a significant impact on who we are.

CHAPTER 1

NANA AND FLINT

It felt like Christmas was coming early. Slowly, the big crate was lowered from the lorry by a small forklift. It couldn't be anything bigger in the narrow streets of Gibraltar. The forklift reached the door of the Gibraltar Museum and could go no further. The box was lowered and now we had to negotiate it by hand, through the entrance and down three steps into a newly prepared exhibition space. It was heavy and it took four to gradually manoeuvre it into its new home. The operation had taken around an hour but it felt like an eternity.

About ten of us were assembled for the operation and now we looked at each other, and the box, in anticipation. My wife Geraldine and my son Stewart, both also scientists, looked at each other and then at me for the signal they had all been waiting for. Stewart took charge and commenced the process of carefully dismantling the crate. The wooden panels were removed only to reveal a bulky parcel covered in bubble wrap and other protective packing. The package had travelled all the way from the Netherlands and no risk of damage could be entertained. For us it simply delayed for a little while longer what we so eagerly wanted to see.

We all saw them at the same time. Two wonderful, life-size sculptures of Neanderthals. Stewart crouched and looked one of the creatures in the eye, and it seemingly reciprocated; luckily,

Figure 1 First contact. Stewart and Flint stare at each other.

I managed to photograph the magic moment that will stay with me forever (Figure 1).

This was all happening in May 2016 but the project had started eighteen months earlier. We had contacted the world-famous forensic artists Adrie and Alfons Kennis and invited them to visit us in Gibraltar to discuss an idea. They jumped at it with an effervescence that we would soon realize characterized them in anything and everything that they did. I have to confess that we weren't quite prepared for that first meeting with Kennis & Kennis[1]. The twins arrived straight from the airport and took immediate charge with a barrage of ideas, all of them absolutely wonderful. Geraldine, Stewart, and I looked at each other and tried to get the occasional word in without much success. The Kennis juggernaut had arrived.

Gibraltar is famous in the world of palaeoanthropology for its Neanderthals. The skull of a female was discovered during quarrying operations as far back as 1848. The discovery predated that in the Neander Valley in Germany[2] by eight years but, at the time, nobody realized the significance of the skull and the German specimen got ahead in the formal naming process some years later. Then, in 1926, an excavation by Cambridge archaeologist Dorothy Garrod[3] revealed the fragmented remains of a second Neanderthal in Gibraltar. This one was a four-year old boy. Gibraltar became synonymous with Neanderthals.

The Gibraltar specimens, somewhat unimaginatively, became known in the palaeoanthropological world as Gibraltar 1 and 2. For years I had stared at these skulls, wondering what these people might have looked like, what their world was like, and how they related to that world and to each other. The response was blank. All I could see were skulls and, sure, they revealed features which I knew were diagnostic of these people, for example the large nasal cavities and eye sockets, the brow ridges and the receding brain case, but that was all. I could not relate to these skulls in any other way. There was no empathy.

Back in 2014 we had been aware of the wonderful work of Kennis & Kennis. Their sculptures of ancient humans were realistic and accurate and they revealed, in their expressions and postures, the flair of the artists themselves. We wanted to put faces to Gibraltar 1 and 2. Stewart was put in charge of making contact; after all he had been the enthusiastic engine driving us forward throughout. Just under two years after this first contact, Stewart was staring a Gibraltar Neanderthal in the face and I was recording the moment.

The intervening period had been spent in discussion with Alfons and Adrie as they sent us sketches with detailed explanations regarding postures and every other detail you can imagine. They had looked at, and studied, living hunter-gatherers. They had a massive catalogue of images which they could draw upon to back up their interpretations. We had a long discussion when they first presented Gibraltar 1 to us. She had her arms folded and crossed with the hands touching the shoulders. It seemed an odd position to us but they showed us images of people in that posture. In their characteristic style they said to me 'where would you put your hands if you didn't have pockets?' and convinced us in the process.

The sculptures were detailed forensic reconstructions, as close to what these Neanderthals looked like as is possible to achieve with today's means. They are a far cry from the ape-like brutish figure reconstructed by Marcellin Boule back in 1907[4]. The reconstructions needed the additional help of physical anthropologists who could work out stature, build, and every detail of the body. After all, we only had two skulls to start off with so we needed advice from the best experts if we were to get it right. There was no question of who to contact. Our friends Christoph Zollikofer and Marcia Ponce de León at the University of Zurich were the best, and it only took a phone call to get them on board. A few weeks after our first meeting with Alfons and Adrie, the Kennis steamroller was heading down the European motorways in the direction of Zurich.

When the sculptures were close to completion, we had several brainstorming sessions to come up with names for Gibraltar 1 and 2. The name for the boy (Gibraltar 2) was easy enough. We decided to call him Flint. Flint is one of the types of rock that Neanderthals used to make tools but it was also the surname of the military officer who discovered the Gibraltar 1 skull in 1848. What about Gibraltar 1? We had asked Alfons and Adrie to make a composition that had the two Neanderthals together. It was a first for them, to put two sculptures together, and it worked. We knew that the Neanderthals whose skulls had been found were probably not even contemporaries but it was a way of telling a story. We decided that the Gibraltar 1 female would be Flint's grandmother, so she became Nana. And so Nana and Flint were born.

The first thing that hits you when you see Nana and Flint is how human they look. The exaggerated features of skull anatomy really fade away once you put skin and flesh to the bone. Nana is a bit on the short side for a human female but is nevertheless well within the range for women today. Their faces and expressions speak of humanity. I have been grappling with the old idea that Neanderthals were somehow inferior cognitively to Modern Humans (our ancestors) for several decades now. To me they were every bit as human as our direct ancestors and I could never fully comprehend the distinctions made on anatomical grounds by palaeoanthropologists—I preferred to focus on the similarities. The behavioural differences which the archaeologists attributed to the two kinds of human were also relatively insignificant and could easily be explained by differences in cultural traditions. Yet the paradigm of Neanderthal inferiority prevailed for a long time and is still at the heart of arguments which are being put forward today by leading students of human origins to explain away the narrative of Neanderthal extinction related to the arrival of superior Modern Humans.

When we opened the new Nana and Flint display in the Gibraltar Museum (Plate 1), we had 1700 people coming to visit the new exhibit on the first day. Most were local people, out of a population of around 30 000. That is the level of interest that Neanderthals generate. It was wonderful to see the reaction of people, particularly children, on first seeing Nana and Flint. Now, everyone talks of Nana and Flint and not of Neanderthals, and certainly not of the anodyne Gibraltar 1 and 2. This is a very important lesson. We had previously seen these humans in a particular way because we had given them a name: Neanderthal. In doing so we created an entity in our minds and the name conditioned how we viewed that being. Skulls and bones simply reinforced their non-humanity. Neanderthal was another way of saying 'other'[5] and from that came the repertoire of connotations related to other. Now, these life-like sculptures with personality rather than bones reinforced a new message, one of humanity.

Why have we grappled for so long with an equivalent name for ourselves? Cro-Magnon never achieved the widespread acceptance that Neanderthal did and instead we went for indecisive terms. First it was Anatomically Modern Humans. When it became clear that the term was incorrect as a number of specimens with apparently anatomically archaic features were in the direct line leading to us, we changed it to Behaviourally Modern Humans[6]. That immediately led us, head first, into the challenge of what it meant to be behaviourally modern[7]. This is the main question that I will try to answer in this book. I will do so by showing how, using the same criteria that archaeologists and palaeo-anthropologists have used to define behavioural modernity, the Neanderthals were just as modern as their contemporaries. Those contemporaries included Behaviourally Modern Humans.

In dealing with this central question of behavioural modernity I will not limit myself to the traditional sources of evidence that have been brought to bear, particularly by archaeologists. These have typically been stone tools, bones including those with cut marks and related evidence of human intervention, and portable and rock art. The distribution of these objects in confined areas, such as caves, or across large geographical areas has also been used as evidence of the structuring of living space or of geographical expansion and exchange networks[8]. Such evidence has been brought to bear in favour of the definition of behavioural modernity.

The old adage that absence of evidence is not evidence of absence is very pertinent here and will be throughout this book. The majority of material culture consists of organic raw materials which are highly perishable. Their absence from the archaeology of most Palaeolithic sites has completely distorted our interpretation of the sites, including the behaviour of the humans who inhabited the sites. This 'missing majority'[9] problem is not trivial but it has not stopped archaeologists from painting a heavily distorted picture of the Palaeolithic. We will see in this book just how distorted this picture really is, especially when it comes to portraying the Neanderthals.

The archaeological evidence which has been put forward as indicative of modern human behaviour was summarized by Cambridge archaeologist Paul Mellars as far back as 1991[10]. He listed seven features that, for him, characterized the transition from the Middle Palaeolithic of the Neanderthals and other archaic humans to the Upper Palaeolithic of the Modern Humans. These were:

1) a change in the way stone tools were made, with a tendency to develop from flakes in the direction of blades[11]; linked to this was an increased standardization in the way in which tools were made—tools were also made using more economical techniques than previously;

2) a simultaneous increase in the variety and complexity of the stone tools which were made;

3) the appearance of complex tools made of bone, antler, and ivory[12];

4) the appearance of new types of technologies with increasing frequency and differences in the way tools were made in different geographical areas;

5) the appearance of beads, pendants, and other 'personal ornaments';

6) the appearance in certain contexts of sophisticated, naturalistic art[13]; and

7) a strong hint of closely associated changes in economic and social organization.

Paul Mellars admitted that these were features that were difficult to demonstrate objectively. The kinds of things he was thinking of were specialized hunting of particular animals, increases in human population density and group size, and also the appearance of structured forms of settlements including huts, tents, and other living structures.

Another renowned Cambridge archaeologist, Colin Renfrew[14], looked at Mellars' list and suggested that this 'human revolution' appeared fairly modest and localized. The naturalistic art was confined to France, Spain, and only a few finds of small sculptures further east in the Czech Republic and in Siberia. It hardly constituted a global event. Renfrew also pointed out that to a non-specialist many of the new features were not overwhelmingly obvious. It took, for example, a specialist to recognize and classify differences in stone tool assemblages between the Middle and the Upper Palaeolithic. For Renfrew, the evidence of the changes associated with the advent of agriculture in the Neolithic[15], much later, was a much more impressive take-off.

In 2007, Mellars[16] conceded that many of the elements that he had argued constituted his human revolution and the change from the Middle to the Upper Palaeolithic in Europe had been found much earlier on the African continent. Nevertheless, he argued, there was sufficient evidence to indicate that the various components had appeared more or less at the same time as a package. For Mellars 'more or less at the same time' meant somewhere between 80 000 and 60 000 years ago. I'll let the reader decide on the accuracy of a time window of 20 000 years for something which happened at the human timescale. So Mellars was simply shifting the time and location of the human revolution but it had still been done by Modern Humans, the ancestors of the people who left Africa and colonized Eurasia. The Neanderthals, confined to Eurasia, never got a look in on this revolution.

Others[17] strongly contested the idea of a revolution and put forward evidence that the various elements of the modern package had appeared gradually in Africa between 280 000 and 40 000 years ago. Of course, this alternative explanation of the archaeological evidence for modern behaviour still confined it to Modern Humans, who were the only humans living in Africa at that time. Evidence of pigment processing was recorded all the way back to 280 000 years ago, and beads from 120 000 years ago, but the naturalistic rock art and the small sculptures—arguably the hallmark of modernity—never showed up in Africa at any point earlier than they did in Europe. The Neanderthals remained out of the picture in all of this African discussion. The debate centred round the time when modern humans became behaviourally modern and whether it all happened at once or gradually. The implication of modern human superiority remained. Once they gained the modern package, these modern humans left Africa to conquer a world which was populated by inferior, archaic humans.

Colin Renfrew has come up with an idea which he calls the Sapient Paradox. He asked what accounted for the huge gap between the arrival of Modern Humans, with their superior cognitive capacity, in Europe 40 000 years ago, and the earliest agricultural revolution, the real human take-off from his perspective, 10 000 years ago? Why had there been a time lag of 30 000 years? If Modern Humans were indeed a genetically distinct and superior entity, why did this cultural and technological explosion not happen sooner? If we take the latest evidence, which points to the earliest modern humans having originated in Africa around 300 000 years ago[18], then the Sapient Paradox becomes even harder to explain.

If to this we add the increasing evidence that Neanderthals, who had originated somewhere in Eurasia at a similar time or even earlier, show practically the entire range of abilities that make up the modern behaviour package, we are left with a conundrum. Now we are faced with a new paradox, which I will call the Neanderthal Paradox: if Neanderthals were really cognitively inferior to Modern Humans why did they survive in the harsh climates of Eurasia for over 300 000 years and why did it take the cognitively superior Modern Humans so long to colonize Eurasia? Is this puzzle real or is it the result of a massive underestimation of the capabilities of Nana, Flint, and their kin?

CHAPTER 2

NEANDERTHALS AND BIRDS

This book is about Neanderthals and birds and the way they interacted with each other. Why should this be interesting and worthy of a book? It all has to do with the modern behavioural package described in Chapter 1, what Neanderthals could or couldn't do, and about new ways of finding evidence that has escaped us with traditional archaeological techniques. For too long absence of evidence has been taken to mean evidence of absence and this could not be further from the truth when it came to Neanderthals and birds, as we are finding out. So why are birds important?

Birds are important because they have been considered to be fast-moving animals which would have been hard for primitive humans, including the Neanderthals, to catch. The zooarchaeologist Mary Stiner formalized this idea in a series of papers[1]. The idea was that Palaeolithic humans would have exploited slow-moving prey before moving onto fast-moving prey. In her definition slow-moving prey meant intertidal molluscs (for example, mussels or limpets) and tortoises. Now, these animals were considered to occur in places in high density which would have attracted humans. Their downfall was that they had low reproductive rates. The result would have been the rapid exhaustion of an area and, presumably, these humans would have then had to move on to the next patch of ground to repeat the operation.

The net effect of this overexploitation was, according to Stiner, the depletion of stocks of slow-moving prey. An outcome of the overexploitation was the decrease in the average size of animals as the largest ones were removed from their habitats. So, in time, slow-moving animals got scarcer and smaller.

Fast-moving prey were essentially birds, rabbits, and hares. These animals had higher reproductive rates than the slower species and were therefore also more resilient. So we would expect that the proportion of fast-moving prey out of the total prey items would increase in a human occupation site with time. Stiner claimed to have found such evidence, which for her also reflected human population pulses. As more people populated the land, so the depletion effect would have increased, and so on. In her view there was a clear jump between the Middle and Upper Palaeolithic (corresponding to Neanderthals and Modern Humans) in the sites which she examined in Italy and Israel. Neanderthals were people who exploited slow-moving prey. Birds, rabbits, and hares were beyond them. Modern Humans, on the other hand, were adept at catching the fast-moving birds, hares, and rabbits. Because these animals reproduced faster than the slow-moving prey, their populations were less subject to depletion and were able to support a higher population of humans than before. So Modern Human abilities to catch fast-moving prey were linked to human population growth.

A similar argument has been developed by another archaeologist, Richard Klein, and his colleagues for a different part of the world—South Africa. There were never any Neanderthals here but Klein has sought to differentiate the earlier Modern Humans of the Middle Stone Age (MSA), roughly contemporary with the Neanderthals, from those who followed in the Late Stone Age (LSA)[2], among whom were the people who undertook the

Out-of-Africa global expansion. Drawing from Stiner's ideas, he has proposed that the MSA people concentrated their activities on slow-moving prey whereas the LSA humans took a wider range of prey including fast-moving prey[3]. This argument has important implications for the study of human origins and modern human behaviour.

Klein argues that a genetic mutation[4] around 50 000 years ago was responsible for the appearance of behaviourally modern humans and assumes that the modern mode of behaviour and geographic expansion were linked. Nobody has found this mutation to date and the link between modernity (as we have already seen, a fuzzy concept) and geographical expansion has not been demonstrated either. You don't need to be a 'genius species' to expand geographically. If you did, then we would expect the animals with the biggest brains or the most sophisticated behaviour to have the widest geographical distributions on the planet[5]. This is evidently not the case: many kinds of animals without brains or with simple ones, not to mention many plants and fungi, are among the most geographically widespread and successful organisms that have ever lived.

Why are these arguments important or relevant when discussing the Neanderthals who were living thousands of miles away from South Africa? They are important because Klein equates the pre-50 000-year old MSA modern humans with the Neanderthals: 'the earliest modern or near-modern Africans were behaviourally (archaeologically) indistinguishable from their nonmodern, Eurasian contemporaries, and it was only after 50 000–40 000 years ago that a major behavioural difference developed.'[6] In other words, all the business about modern behavioural packages, slow- and fast-moving prey exploitation, and the like are really about putting our ancestors of 50 000 years ago on a pedestal at the expense of not just the Neanderthals, but of their very own ancestors.

Material culture does not necessarily equate to behavioural capacities and cognition. If it did, then a scientist from the future looking at the material culture associated with my generation and that of my grandparents would conclude that they were cognitively inferior to me. So would the people of the Renaissance, or the Romans and the Greeks, or the people of the Neolithic for that matter. We simply cannot get a collection of artefacts (already biased against perishable items) from a site and have the audacity of translating that evidence into a measure of level of cognition on the part of the makers or owners of those artefacts. Yet that is exactly what archaeologists have done in order to tell the story of human origins and the demise of the Neanderthals.

The arguments about modern human cognitive superiority which Klein and others have been putting forward for decades are part of a narrative of human origins and evolution. The story reaches its climax with the inevitable arrival of our ancestors and the elimination of all humans that they came across. In an excellent book on stone tools and human evolution[7], archaeologist John Shea discusses narratives in human evolution and their inherent problems: 'Stories, or "narrative explanations", are cultural universals as old as history itself, and probably much, much older. Early palaeoanthropologists expressed their hypotheses about human evolution in narrative frameworks, and the practice continues to this day. Narratives force one to arrange complex evolutionary processes into simple linear chains of cause and effect. All evolutionary narratives of human origins begin with the oldest evidence, evidence about which geological attrition alone guarantees we know the least. Interpretive errors made at the beginning of such a narrative make all subsequent interpretations in that narrative wrong too. Narrative explanations for events that took place over geological/evolutionary timescales are intrinsically likely to be wrong.'

Shea points out that hypotheses about human evolution that are presented as narratives can appear to provide explanations of the facts we know at any given moment, but they lack predictive power. So every new discovery comes as a surprise, as a game changer. As a result, archaeologists constantly tinker with these narratives to try to accommodate newly discovered evidence. The narratives become increasingly complex and difficult to understand.

John Shea's view summarizes the current picture of human origins beautifully. We saw in Chapter 1 how the idea of a human revolution that took place in Europe around 40 000 years ago was tinkered with when it became obvious that most of the components of the human revolution predated that key date and were found on another continent. But the narrative was not changed. Instead the evidence was massaged gently to fit into the existing narrative: Once upon a time all humans were primitive. We call the primitive people of Eurasia the Neanderthals. We call the primitive people of Africa Archaic Modern Humans. At some stage in the story, a miraculous mutation, that we are yet to find, made the African Archaic Modern Humans suddenly Behaviourally Modern. As a result of this behavioural modernity the human population grew. This population growth led to improved efficiency in the hunting of animals. This population growth also led to the diversification of the human diet to include previously untapped foods, especially fast-moving prey such as rabbits, hares, and birds. As a result of this behavioural modernity and consequent population growth, these humans expanded from

Africa and colonized the world. In the process it was inevitable that the cognitively inferior primitive peoples of the world were replaced by the superior Behaviourally Modern Humans.

We identify behavioural modernity, which is equated to cognitive superiority, through material culture (i.e. archaeology). Having accepted the premise that material culture equates to cognition, which is clearly false, we define the elements of the behaviourally modern package. We listed these in Chapter 1 and we have added those which the zooarchaeologists have considered important in this chapter.

So now we know why birds are important to understanding the Neanderthals. According to the conventional view described so far, Neanderthals should not be taking birds systematically and regularly, since birds are fast-moving prey, and Neanderthals lacked the technology and know-how to catch and exploit birds. In these ways Neanderthals were inferior to the Modern Humans who were able to do such things.

Before moving on to the birds, we need to clarify some important points that put the whole idea of modernity and the modern human expansion and subsequent replacement of the Neanderthals into serious doubt. In the first place the date of 50 000 years ago for the big change in our behaviour that led to our global expansion cannot be countenanced any longer. The date might have matched the arrival of modern humans into Europe but it does not match what happened elsewhere. There is now clear evidence that modern humans were in Sumatra, South-east Asia, somewhere between 73 000 and 63 000 years ago[8]. The arrival of modern humans in Australia is now thought to have taken place by 65 000 years ago[9]. In southern China evidence of modern humans is even older, dating to at least 80 000 years ago and possibly as much as 120 000 years ago[10]. This clearly means that humans left Africa long before 50 000 years ago. A conservative estimate for the departure would put it around 85 000 years ago but it may well have been even earlier than this. And even as this book was in production, the presence of Modern Humans in the Arabian Peninsula was confirmed by around 85 000 years ago[11]. The earliest modern humans in Europe, on the other hand, are claimed to date to between 45 000 and 40 000 years ago[12], but the evidence leaves a lot to be desired, as we shall see later in this book. For now, let's accept that these estimates are correct.

The big question then is why did it take modern humans so long to reach Europe (some 40 000 years if we use the conservative date of 85 000 years ago), considerably longer than the time to reach South-east Asia and Australia which were much further away? I provided the answer in 2014[13]: the Neanderthals kept the modern humans out of Europe. The paper published in 2015[10] revealing the old age of the southern Chinese modern humans seems to have reached exactly the same conclusion. The important point is that, if it was indeed the case that Neanderthals kept modern humans out, then the story of Modern Human cognitive superiority must be wrong. This is the Neanderthal Paradox which I referred to in Chapter 1.

The next big question mark has to do with what happened when Neanderthals and Modern Humans met. It is now clear that the two interbred[14] and that non-Africans today carry between 1.8 and 2.6 per cent Neanderthal DNA. The proportion is higher in East Asians (2.3–2.6 per cent) than in Western Eurasians (1.8–2.4 per cent). Not every individual today carries the same Neanderthal genes and an estimate suggests that up to 20 per cent of the Neanderthal genome still survives today[15]. Even the staunchest defender of the differences between Neanderthals and Modern Humans must concede that those differences must not have appeared that great in real time and on the ground when the two met.

When the first evidence of Neanderthal–Modern Human inter-breeding appeared in 2010[16] opinions were quick to follow about where and when such interbreeding took place, what it meant, and how widespread it had been[17]. It was yet another example of the tinkering that goes on when something radically new is discovered which doesn't fit according to plan.

Results continue to be published and are revealing that, contrary to the views of critics who favoured the Neanderthal–Modern Human distinction, interbreeding was widespread and spanned a long period of time. Recent estimates suggest that exchanges of genetic material may, on the one hand, have been taking place as far back as 100 000 years ago[18] and, on the other, as recently as 37 000 years ago[19].

The key issue regarding Neanderthal capabilities has ultimately to do with cognition and neurobiology. A recent study[20] looked at a large number of healthy individuals of European descent. Researchers found that there was an important connection between genetic material originating with the Neanderthals, and carried by people today, and cranial and brain morphology. The authors of the study concluded that 'the associations between Neanderthal sequence variation and co-localized skull and brain morphology in modern humans engender an enduring, living footprint of *H. neanderthalensis*—a residual echo of shared, intimate history with a fallen lineage close to our own.' To this they added 'we suggest that Neanderthal gene flow into modern humans is not only of evolutionary interest, but may also be functional in the living *H. sapiens* brain.'

Three main aspects of Paul Mellars' modern human package, with the subsequent brushstrokes provided by Mary Stiner and Richard Klein, will occupy us for the rest of this book. They are: the appearance of beads, pendants, and other 'personal ornaments'; the appearance in certain contexts of sophisticated, naturalistic art; and changes in economic and social organization.

We will seek to find evidence that Neanderthals could do these things when they were supposed not to. Our most recent work is revealing just how important birds are to this story. Birds have come to the rescue of the Neanderthals.

CHAPTER 3

LESSONS FROM THE ARCTIC

The alarm rings at three in the morning. It's dark outside. The only way to deal with this kind of situation and avoid going back to sleep, which is the natural temptation, is to get up quickly and switch on the light. That has the added effect of waking up my son, Stewart, who is sharing a room with me. For a few seconds I'm disconcerted: everything is new and strange and I have forgotten where I am or how I got here. This all quickly gives way to a brand new set of emotions with the realization that one of Nature's special treats awaits us.

A hot shower always helps the process of waking up. Quickly we don three layers of insulating clothing as we struggle to fit into the bright red, single-piece, Norwegian lifeguard outfits which have been specially provided for us. We try to go down to the hotel lobby as silently as possible but it's not easy when you feel like a Michelin Man with a heavy rucksack on your back. Downstairs a familiar face awaited us. It's funny how we had only met our guide Petri, a friendly Finnish ornithologist, the day before, yet in a world in which everything was new a day spent with Petri had made him almost a life-long friend.

We had left Gibraltar at six in the morning two days earlier. After a drive of just over an hour we were checking in at Malaga Airport on a four-and-a-half hour flight to Helsinki. From Helsinki we boarded a second plane to Ivalo in Finnish Lapland, beyond the Arctic Circle, where Petri was waiting with a smile when we eventually landed just before ten at night. He had driven 500 kilometres on icy roads from his home town of Oulu in western Finland for the rendezvous. It was late and we were all tired but we still had an hour-and-a-half's drive ahead of us before we could get to bed in a rustic lodge in the village of Kaamanen. We were glad we had Petri with us. We had contemplated at one stage simply hiring a car and finding our own way but it made every sense to go with someone who knew the lie of the land. Driving on icy roads across the Taiga forest[1] late at night, with no more than a few scattered villages and hamlets on the way, is not something for beginners.

We eventually arrived at the delightful wooden lodge at Kaamanen, having been treated to a wonderful display of the Aurora Borealis along the way. It was late and everyone had gone to bed, though not before kindly leaving hot soup and some snacks for us to devour.

Kaamanen village has around 200 inhabitants dedicated largely to reindeer husbandry. We didn't meet many of them the next morning but we were welcomed by one in particular. I was finishing breakfast when Stewart, who had popped out to see the scenery, came calling me and Petri to come outside quickly. A reindeer, with a single antler, had ventured out of the forest and seemed not to mind our presence. We soon realized why. Our host Mika came out with some bread. He gave some to Stewart and the reindeer took it from his hand. After a long while of close-up photography the animal left as stealthily as it had come and merged once again into the Taiga.

That brief encounter brought home a message that we had been advocating for some years and which will be a key part of

this book: in interpreting the past and the abilities of our ancestors in the remote Pleistocene[2] we have not given due weight to
the myriad interrelationships that would have existed between
humans and animals. We have focused our attention on the
study of archaeology and palaeoanthropology but we have not
done natural history. Our distant ancestors were the best natural
historians that ever lived and we will not understand them fully if
we limit our research to the study of skulls, stone tools, or butchery marks on bones. We have to understand them from within by
getting into the field and observing the animals which they also
saw and hunted, and in some cases probably revered. We will not
find this out by studying field guides or handbooks; we will only
do it if we are prepared to get muddy, frozen, or sun-baked as circumstances might dictate.

We are lucky that, even though many of the mammal species[3]
that our ancestors saw are now extinct and beyond our reach, the
same is not the case with birds. With the exception of the great
auk[4], which we will have the chance to meet later in this book, the
birds which our ancestors knew in the Pleistocene are still around
today. Despite this wonderful window of opportunity, of being
able to observe and study animals which were known to people
as far back as 100 000 years ago (and in many cases well beyond),
nobody seems to have taken up the challenge. We took it up over
a decade ago and this book is the story of what we found. But it
is also the story of how we went about carrying out our research.
Scientific papers typically have a methods section which is usually
a dry account which few people, other than specialists, ever read.
Only too often books present results and discussion but don't go
into the detail, often anecdotal, of the things that happened along
the way. Here I want to tell also of the unimaginable joy spent

in the field among birds which were once the neighbours of the Neanderthals and their kin. As an ornithologist who discovered a second passion in the study of the Neanderthals, this has been an enriching and fulfilling endeavour.

That was precisely why we were in Finland. Not because we expected to have close encounters with reindeer even though one had reinforced our thinking quite by chance but because we wanted to find, see, and understand the behaviour of a bird that frequently appeared in Neanderthal and other human Pleistocene sites across Eurasia: the long-tailed duck[5].

Kaamanen Lodge is renowned in the birding fraternity for its bird feeder. Food is regularly placed outside the lodge and the birds that dare attempt to survive the cold winters in this part of the Taiga find a welcome source of energy here. My experience here, as in other parts of the frozen north, be it Greenland, Scandinavia, or Canada, is that hungry birds will lower their guard significantly and become very approachable. You don't need a hide or any other form of cover to get within three or four metres of the birds.

The Kaamanen feeding station was no exception. Even though we had a long drive ahead, we decided to spend a couple of hours at the feeder to see and photograph what came in. It did not disappoint. Siberian tits and Siberian jays were the stars for us as these were birds of the Taiga which we would not expect to encounter at home, nor indeed anywhere much further south in Europe. Here, at 69°N, well within the Arctic Circle and, in early March, with a temperature of −15°C, they ruled the roost. There were other birds which were more familiar to us, amazingly surviving at the edge of their range: greenfinches, great and willow tits, and even house sparrows pluckily took seeds from their northern counterparts and from the red squirrels that delighted with their aerial displays between the pine trees, shaking clumps of snow into fine dust in the process.

The Kaamanen feeder inadvertently showed us another little field experiment of the kind that we had been interested in for some time now. There were some birds which were specialists of these climates and forests. Take them out of here and they would not survive long. These birds are good indicators of particular climatic and ecological conditions. Find their remains in a Pleistocene cave and you have a pretty good idea of what was going on outside the cave at the time. The remains of the Siberian jay have been found in Pleistocene sites in Germany and France and we can be quite confident in inferring that the Taiga forest had migrated south to those latitudes at the time.

Find a greenfinch or a great tit instead and they tell you very little. These birds span the entire latitudinal breadth of Europe and are at home in a variety of woodland and woodland edge habitats. They are remarkable as generalists that have been able to cope with most climatic situations which have been thrown their way but we are likely to learn more from a Siberian tit than we are from a great tit.

The bird that really excited us at Kaamanen was another finch—the pine grosbeak (Figure 2). The first thing that strikes you when you see this bird is its size. It weighs anything up to 65 grams, between two and three times the size of the greenfinches (themselves large by finch standards). The bright red males stood out against the green of the pine needles and they also, tamely, came down to the feeder in full view of us standing close by. Why should this bird have thrilled us so much?

The pine grosbeak is another resident of the Taiga, although some populations do perform short-distance movements in the winter. Their behaviour is said to be irruptive. In some years large

Figure 2 Pine Grosbeak at Kaamanen Village, Finland.

numbers descend on areas which are not part of the home range, and strip down rowan and other trees of all their fruit and seeds. Even so, the pine grosbeak is rare in Western Europe. There are no historical records for the Iberian Peninsula at all[6].

For a long time we had been puzzled by the presence of pine grosbeaks in Pleistocene sites across Europe, right down into northern Spain. These were not isolated cases either, since bird remains appear in several archaeological contexts[7] at some sites, indicating that they had been there more than once. In terms of Taiga birds, Pleistocene pine grosbeaks had wandered much further afield than Siberian jays. Or, at least, they had found their way into caves more frequently.

A number of the sites where this bird was found were intriguingly associated with the Neanderthals. This did not mean, of course, that the Neanderthals had caught or eaten them. Finding direct proof of Neanderthal capture of birds is not easy and will occupy us later in this book. But it should not stop us thinking about why the two seem to be associated, and Kaamanen gave us an important clue.

As we watched these chunky birds, we remarked to Petri how struck we were by their tameness. He told us a story that left us with our mouths wide open. When the pine grosbeaks feed on the rowan berries they are so intent on what they are doing that you can easily catch them with a long stick with a string noose at the end. You simply put the noose round the bird's neck and you have caught it. The technique was used for catching birds to place metal rings round their legs to study their movements, but Petri told us that the technique had been borrowed from the old people who used to catch them for food in Finland. The practice of catching pine grosbeaks may have been related to their apparent innocence or tameness, possibly because these birds had been born in the Taiga forests of Russia and were naïve regarding humans. In Western Europe catching pine grosbeaks was apparently common during irruption years[8].

Maybe catching pine grosbeaks went back much deeper in time, all the way to the Pleistocene. It would not have required particularly sophisticated technology and what tools were used were likely to have been made of perishable, archaeologically invisible, materials. But most important of all, it would have required guile.

It was time to be on our way. We had a long drive ahead which would take us north into Norway and the Varanger Peninsula to the town of Batsfjord on the shores of the Barents Sea. We set off through the beautiful pine forest and snow scenery of the Taiga forest. The long drive gave us time to chat with Petri who was curious to know of our interest in the long-tailed duck. Most birders and photographers went to Batsfjord to get the sea duck but the long-tailed duck was not necessarily first on their agenda. The main species which were sought after were the king and Steller's eiders which were real specialities up there. We explained.

The long-tailed duck is a species that we have found in a number of archaeological contexts associated with Neanderthals in Gibraltar. Yet, the long-tailed duck rarely reaches the Iberian Peninsula in winter today and then mostly to the northern coasts[6]. The quantity of remains of this bird in Gibraltar suggested to us that it was once common down there, perhaps in the winter. We wanted to see these birds in their prime winter habitat today and the Varanger Peninsula was an obvious, if remote, choice.

The archaeological contexts in which the bones of long-tailed duck had been found in Gibraltar were in caves, especially two large sea caves on the eastern side of the Rock: Gorham's and Vanguard Caves. They had also been found in a small rock shelter at the base of the North Face of the Rock known as the Devil's Tower Rock Shelter. This latter site had become famous because of the discovery of the skull of a four-year old Neanderthal child (Chapter 1) alongside stone tools and the bones of many animals, including the long-tailed duck.

The main caves in Gibraltar were Gorham's and Vanguard and we had been excavating them since 1989. Within the caves we found the remains of Neanderthal camp fires, stone tools, butchered animals; we had everything that allowed us to build up a picture of Neanderthal ecology as never before. The emerging picture was that from 127 000 years ago, when we had the first evidence of Neanderthal presence in the caves, until the last Neanderthals that survived there around 32 000 years ago, when the climate in Gibraltar had been relatively mild, in spite of Europe being under the grip of an Ice Age. None of the Ice Age mammals—woolly mammoth, woolly rhinoceros, musk ox, reindeer—ever reached this far south. So why the duck?

As for the Neanderthals, they had lived across Eurasia from at least 300 000 years ago. Gibraltar was the south-westernmost part of their range. Africa, only 21 kilometres away and visible from Gorham's Cave, had never, as far as we knew, been populated by Neanderthals. For over a decade we had been struggling to overturn the image of the Neanderthal as a brutish, hairy, ape-like creature—the archetypal caveman. We had been building up a case that showed the Neanderthals to be capable of sophisticated behaviours, comparable in all respects to the later modern humans who had arrived in Europe from Africa around 40 000 years ago.

Among the behaviours which the Neanderthals had been denied was the ability to catch birds. That skill came with our intelligent ancestors and was brought into Eurasia by them when they arrived from Africa. Our work indicated that this was not the case. We were picking many flaws in arguments which, it seemed to us, were being put forward with little understanding of the ecology and behaviour of the birds themselves. We had realized also that the best way to get a handle on the problem was to combine the results from the work in our caves and others across Eurasia with an intimate knowledge of the birds themselves. If we could understand the ecology and behaviour of the different species of birds found in the caves from the perspective of a human hunter, then we might begin to understand their relationship to the Neanderthals. Studying birds today would never tell us exactly how Neanderthals related to them but what it would do was give us insights into the possible and the impossible. We would be able to start producing a Neanderthal natural history.

Finding the long-tailed duck was our current stage in a long process; after all we had already identified 151 species[9] of birds in our caves alone. This amounted to 30 per cent of all European species in just these caves. That had to mean something. By the time we were coming to the end of our conversation we were reaching Batsfjord, having stopped for lunch on the Finnish–Norwegian border and having delighted at the habitat transitions as we went north: the Taiga soon gave way to dwarf birch forest which in turn gave way to snow and ice-covered tundra. After an early dinner, by our standards at least, we went to bed as we had an appointment with some long-tailed ducks at three the following morning.

CHAPTER 4

THE LONG-TAILED DUCK

I never thought I'd find a balaclava useful but when you are going along a cold Norwegian fjord in a rigid-hulled inflatable boat (RIB) in the dark with a temperature of −19°C plus wind chill, it becomes an indispensable item of clothing. We had left Gibraltar, over 4000 kilometres to the south as the crow flies and with a mid-day temperature of +20°C, two days earlier. The almost 40 degree contrast spanned the latitudinal width of Europe. My thoughts on the climatic contrasts from south to north in Europe and how they would have affected Neanderthals and birds soon came to a halt as we reached a large cube that was floating on the water—this floating hide was going to be home for the next eight hours.

Ørjan is a Norwegian who lives in Batsfjord and runs two floating hides where you can observe Arctic sea duck at close quarters. We met him at four in the morning by a small pier just outside the town where he kept his RIBs. After the customary introductions and greetings we boarded the RIB, with great caution as the jetty and the RIB itself had a covering of compacted snow and ice. It was on this that we sat as we were driven to the floating hide. Getting from the RIB onto the narrow ledge by the entrance to the hide was equally hazardous as we transferred our equipment and then ourselves. A slip and a fall onto the icy water would not have been a good idea.

The hide was surprisingly spacious, at least by the standards we were used to elsewhere, even though we couldn't stand fully upright. These hides are essentially boxes with openings from which you can observe and photograph birds at close quarters without disturbing them. These particular hides had several openings, some at shoulder level and others right by the floor. The floor had a covering of matting to provide some insulation. When we arrived the openings were all shut and, as it was still night time, we saw our way around with head torches. The idea of arriving so early was so that the birds got no wind of our presence inside when they arrived and, as Ørjan left, we now had a long wait in the dark until first light and the birds.

'ah-oo-GAH' is how the *Handbook of the Birds of the Western Palearctic*[1] describes the loud yodelling courtship cry of the male long-tailed duck. It doesn't really do it justice but, then again, it's virtually impossible to describe the sound in words so it's as close as we can get. Two things happened before we had sufficient light to see outside: one was the distinctive sound of flapping wings combined with the rushing noise of fast-moving water and the other was the unmistakable haunting 'ah-oo-GAH'. Sitting there in the dark and listening to these sounds made me think that sometime in the remote past a Neanderthal somewhere, perhaps all the way south in Gibraltar, had had a similar experience. Judging from the presence of long-tailed ducks in several Neanderthal sites across Atlantic coastal Europe, it probably hadn't been an isolated experience either.

The movements of long-tailed ducks down the Atlantic seaboard of Europe in the Pleistocene are not a trivial matter when trying to understand the behaviour and geographical distribution of the Neanderthals in Europe. For the Neanderthals, the mild and humid climate of Western Europe was a blessing[2]. For tens of thousands of years it offered them ecological conditions that were optimal: woodland with rich food resources and a plentiful supply of fresh water. To the north and east, the arid continental climate restricted the woodland and water was harder to come by. The long-tailed ducks signal to us how the optimal conditions shifted and were restricted as cold and arid conditions advanced into Western Europe from time to time. The fact that birds are able to respond much quicker to climate change than the large mammals also means that we are able to pick up smaller-scale changes in climate with birds. That, in turn, would allow us to understand the Neanderthal response to climate changes.

For example, it would take several generations at least for a population of woolly mammoths to expand across Europe in response to climate change. Many would perish in the home grounds as conditions became severe, and others would slowly enter new grounds as these became favourable. Long-tailed ducks, on the other hand, could quickly shift their breeding and wintering areas to the south and west as continental climates descended upon their traditional areas. If the climatic deterioration was relatively short-lived, say covering a few decades, then we might not even detect the mammoth range shift at all; by the time they had got going the climate would have improved again and they would return. The ducks, on the other hand, would leave us a clear signal and that is what we find in such places as Gibraltar.

My son Stewart has been trying to figure out, as part of his PhD thesis, whether the Arctic and boreal birds which got all the way down to Gibraltar at the time of the Neanderthals were a random assortment of the species available or, instead, a select few. If the latter, then did these species share features that might give

us clues as to what might have been going on? I may have inadvertently given a clue as to the answer to this question when I described
the pine grosbeak and its behaviour in Chapter 3. This species of the
Taiga forest has never reached the latitude of Gibraltar, even though
it had spread widely across Europe during the Pleistocene. Stewart's
analysis showed precisely that not all Arctic and boreal birds reached
Gibraltar's latitude; those that did had something in common.

Before we jump straight into the birds, let's have a look at the
mammals and see what they show us about the relationship
between them, their ecology, and the Neanderthals. As an undergraduate reading zoology I had been taught that it was always a
useful technique to compare and contrast different animals as it
would help us tease out key aspects of their biology. So this analysis
of the mammals will position us well when we then examine the
birds themselves. In trying to understand the Neanderthals, their
world, and their extinction, I have argued[2] that it was the expansion of the treeless steppe-tundra across their European territory
which led to the geographical fragmentation of their populations and the consequent decline in numbers. The reason was that
Neanderthals were best suited to ambush hunting large mammals with the use of thrusting spears[3]. To successfully apply this
method they needed the cover provided by trees. As trees disappeared from the landscape the Neanderthals attempted, as intelligent humans, to adapt, but their bulky physique could not change
fast enough and they went into decline. Or so I thought until now.

One of the problems with this interpretation, which has wor-
ried me for some time, is the presence of Neanderthal sites across
Central Europe with a steppe-tundra fauna[4]. I have considered
that these might be sites where Neanderthals were living on the
edge and barely surviving, but it does require further thought

34

and I decided to see exactly how many Neanderthal sites across Europe had steppe-tundra animals and how many did not. It was important in this analysis[5] to determine the location of these sites to see exactly where the Neanderthals met these animals.

The two species which appeared overwhelmingly most frequently in Neanderthal sites were horse and red deer[6]. These animals were also geographically widespread, from Russia in the east right down to Gibraltar in the south-west. They are not animals of the steppe-tundra but occupy a range of habitats from fairly open country to closed woodland and would have been ideal prey for the ambush-hunting Neanderthals. So their appearance at Neanderthal sites is in keeping with expectation and says nothing about Neanderthals venturing onto the steppe-tundra.

What species come next down the list? Three species appear in approximately half of all the sites which I examined, and here it starts to get interesting. The reindeer is third on the list closely followed by wolf and spotted hyena. This unusual combination may appear odd but spotted hyenas were once widespread across Eurasia[7]; they were generalized hunter-scavengers and the herds of large herbivores, reminiscent of today's Serengeti, offered plenty of opportunities for them. Wolves would also have thrived, and they too were present right across Europe. What about reindeer? Their presence in half of the Neanderthal sites might, in the first instance, implicate the Neanderthals in the steppe-tundra landscapes that I have suggested were really not ideal for them.

When we look at the geographical distribution of these reindeer sites we find a striking difference from those species which we have looked at so far. Neanderthal sites with reindeer were widespread across the Central European Plain, from the United Kingdom east across to Hungary and the Czech Republic. Reindeer lived further north and east but they don't seem to have been linked with Neanderthals. So the first observation is that Neanderthals were mainly (or even exclusively) associated with reindeer in Europe. If we then look at the pattern in more detail we see that most sites were in France, virtually at the extreme west of the reindeer range. The large number of well-studied French sites is probably biasing our observations and making the Neanderthal–reindeer correlation disproportionately high. Reindeer penetrated into northern Spain and Italy but the Neanderthals do not seem to have been attracted to them here and they certainly had no access to them deep in the south—reindeer never reached Gibraltar.

There is an incorrect assumption that I need to put right before we proceed. In Chapter 1, I described the brief visit of a reindeer at Kaamanen Lodge. It came out of the Taiga forest and returned to it. There was no Tundra anywhere in the vicinity. So this reindeer was not indicating Tundra. In fact, reindeer are highly adaptable and live in Taiga forest as well as Tundra[8]. The forest animals live in smaller groups than their Tundra relatives and they are sedentary, contrasting with the long migrations of the Tundra herds. It means that reindeer presence in Central and Western Europe, where they do not occur today, could reflect either open Tundra or closed Taiga forest. Can we separate out the Neanderthal sites to see whether they are Tundra (which would implicate the Neanderthals in open country) or Taiga forest? This is difficult using only lists of species but I had an idea and it certainly gives us an important clue.

What other mammals occur alongside reindeer in Neanderthal sites? I looked for four species in particular. Red deer and aurochs are temperate-climate animals that can live in many different situations, usually with some woodland cover, but not in extreme cold and treeless landscapes. Woolly mammoth and woolly rhinoceros were the archetypal species of the steppe-tundra. If we find them alongside reindeer it must indicate open, treeless, habitats. So I separated out Neanderthal sites only with reindeer, woolly mammoth, and woolly rhino (steppe-tundra) from those with these steppe-tundra animals and also red deer and aurochs (forest and steppe-tundra both present) and those with only red deer and aurochs (woodland and forest).

Over a third of the sites only had red deer and aurochs and this suggested that the reindeer were forest animals. All these sites were in France at the south-westernmost, presumably climatically mildest, end of the Neanderthal and reindeer range. Almost 40 per cent of the sites had all the species, suggesting a mix of habitats and reindeer that could be forest or Tundra dwellers. Around two thirds of the sites were in France but there were sites also further north and east where climates may have been more rigorous. Only a quarter of the sites could be attributed to Tundra and only 40 per cent were in France, the remainder being to the north and east. So, it seems that Neanderthals may only rarely have exploited Tundra animals after all and possibly then only in situations where woodland was not far away.

Despite this result we cannot ignore the fact that some Neanderthal sites do give a clear signal of steppe-tundra conditions. The same happens when we look at the birds associated with Neanderthal sites. At Gibraltar, we find snowy owls, brent geese, and Arctic sea duck, among them the long-tailed duck. These are all species of the Tundra and its lakes, so does this mean that the Tundra, having spread across Western Europe and south across the Pyrenees, reached all the way down to Gibraltar, the southernmost part of Europe? This conclusion would seem to make sense a priori but accepting it would leave us with a paradox. Why have we never found the remains of Tundra mammals—reindeer, woolly mammoth, woolly rhinoceros—in Gibraltar?

What we have instead is a mammal community that signals warm, wooded conditions throughout. Spanish ibex, red deer, aurochs, wild boar, and horse are not Tundra animals and they were found repeatedly alongside the Neanderthals here, as we would expect, and they were living in Mediterranean climatic conditions where olive and stone pine trees[9] dominated the landscape. The entire sequence of vegetation in the Gibraltar caves, inferred from pollen and charcoal, does not include a single plant species that would have been typical of the steppe-tundra[10].

The paradox gets more complicated when we find that the long-tailed ducks are found alongside the remains of birds which would be at home in the warm Mediterranean climate of Gibraltar today[11]. So what was going on? This is one of the questions which Stewart has been looking at and he has come up with some very interesting and convincing results. In a nutshell, the arrival of long-tailed ducks at Gibraltar has more to do with climatic conditions elsewhere than at Gibraltar itself.

The reason we were able to observe long-tailed ducks in the Varanger Peninsula, within the Arctic Circle, in winter was that the remaining trickle that started off in tropical Caribbean waters as the Gulf Stream and became the North Atlantic Drift reaches all the way up here, to the Barents Sea. It keeps the waters ice-free and the sea duck from right across northern Siberia throng here. Go further east along this latitude into Russia and the sea freezes in the winter. During the Second World War, Allied convoys from the United States, Canada, and Great Britain brought millions of tons of supplies to the Russian ports of Murmansk and Archangel, very close to where we observed the sea duck. These were dangerous operations—known as the Murmansk Run—and many lost their lives, but these operations could not have happened without the same moderating influence of the ocean currents that brought the sea duck here. The ports further east were closed to shipping in the winter just as they are barred to the birds today.

Go back thirty or more thousand years and we are heading for the height of the last Ice Age. You would find the encroaching ice sheets engulfing much of the Scandinavian Peninsula and the British Isles. Sea ice covers the ocean and there is little scope for anything to carve out an existence here, even in the summer. The Tundra has shifted south of the ice and, as we have seen, has come down into Germany and large areas of France. If the conditions at the time had persisted to the present day then the Varanger Peninsula and the Russian ports would be isolated and inaccessible and there would never have been a Murmansk Run.

The result is that the nesting areas of birds like the long-tailed duck had to have shifted southwards. Instead of breeding in the High Arctic these birds would have now found available nesting habitats somewhere in southern Britain or France. In winter, the migrations which today take them from deep Siberia to the mild Atlantic coasts of Norway and even down to Scotland (where I have observed large numbers of long-tailed ducks in the sheltered bays on the island of Unst in Shetland) would have been replaced by movements down the Atlantic coasts of France, Spain, and Portugal and all the way to Gibraltar and even into the Mediterranean Sea. It didn't just affect the long-tailed ducks.

There is a site on the northern coast of Spain[12], on the shore of the Bay of Biscay, where sea duck that are even hardier than the long-tailed duck turned up. At Varanger we observed two other sea duck—Steller's and king eiders. These species are so tough that this was about as far south as they would venture. They are rarities anywhere in Europe today and then only seen in the winter. So even they were forced on to the coasts of southern Britain, France, and northern Spain during the last Ice Age. As I was revising the chapters of this book the amazing news came that remains of Steller's eiders had been found in Gorham's Cave and we could add this High Arctic species to our list. It reinforced the image of a Varanger that existed once upon a time at Gibraltar (Figure 3).

When Stewart analysed the 'cold' bird species which got all the way down to Gibraltar, and those which didn't, he had an eureka moment. He came rushing into my laboratory excitedly waving a printout with what appeared to be long lists of bird species. It didn't take me long to understand what he was showing me—the results were stunningly clear, as were their implications. The birds

Figure 3 Steller's eiders and long-tailed ducks in Varanger today.

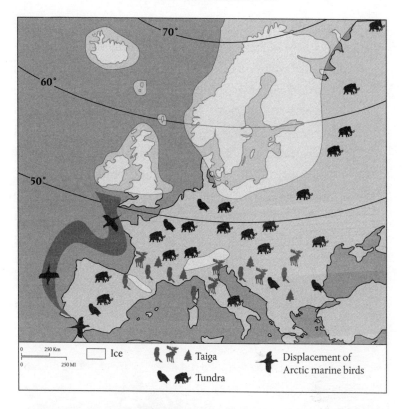

Figure 4 Map illustrating the southern limit of the Taiga during cold events in the Pleistocene. The Tundra is generally to the north of the Taiga but leapfrogs it at high altitude in the Mediterranean peninsulas, especially Iberia where the cold fauna penetrated the Central Tablelands. Arctic marine birds and some Tundra birds reached Gibraltar as a result of displacement from the north.

that did reach Gibraltar during the Late Pleistocene were Arctic birds typical of coastal areas and Tundra. The forest birds of the Taiga had not moved south as much and so they had been leap-frogged by the birds from further north.

As conditions across Europe got colder during the glaciations, the northern forest belts migrated southwards and penetrated well into the Balkan Peninsula, less so into the Italian Peninsula, and even less into the Iberian Peninsula. These forests were located, as we would expect, south of the Tundra that spread across much of Western and Central Europe. But in Iberia the Tundra reappeared to the south of the Taiga forest on the exposed and windswept Central Tablelands[13]. Altitude was the key factor which overturned the effect of latitude and this gave a window of opportunity for woolly mammoths and other members of the cold fauna to penetrate deep into Iberia. Here, the Taiga forest stayed north of the Tundra, a situation which has no parallel today (Figure 4).

That was well enough when explaining the absence of the Taiga birds, like the pine grosbeaks, from Gibraltar but the Tundra never reached the south of Iberia and certainly not right down to Gibraltar in the deep south and at sea level. The list of birds that did reach Gibraltar was not long but the species were surprisingly similar in ecology. We could see two distinct groups: one was the sea duck of which the long-tailed duck was representative and the other was Tundra birds of prey. The snowy owl was the most eye-catching species in the latter group. It was time to go in search of the White Ghost.

CHAPTER 5

THE WHITE GHOST

Southern Ontario in Canada may not be as far north as Varanger but, in February, it's just as white and cold with temperatures reaching −30°C. Twenty-five degrees of latitude separate the two and we are in open country somewhere between Ottawa and Montreal, at a latitude similar to Bordeaux in south-west France. The difference is that while Bordeaux is under the influence of the warm waters of the North Atlantic Drift, Ontario is away from the coast and has a continental climate which, in winter, is heavily influenced by winds coming down from the Arctic.

Stewart and I were flying into Montreal one night in February when the worst storm of the winter hit the area. After two uncomfortable attempts to land in the middle of a snow blizzard, the pilot decided to divert to Toronto where the worst of the storm had passed. Landing there was less problematic but we were then stranded inside the aircraft for five hours as ground crews struggled to get us out of the plane, the frozen tarmac presenting all kinds of dilemmas for the handling of an unexpected arrival. If one thought crossed my mind above all others it was how different conditions were at these latitudes in North America compared to the relatively benign climate of Western Europe at the same latitude.

The inconvenience, which delayed our work by twenty-four hours, curiously primed us to a clear understanding of why we were here and why we couldn't do something similar practically any-where in Europe, not even in the far north at Varanger. The next day we took a train to Ottawa and a hired car to our target site which to us seemed to be in the middle of nowhere, driving on frozen country roads and tracks to get there. We had come here with one specific target in mind and it was somewhat disconcerting to think that we could have achieved our objective without moving out of Gibraltar had we been living there at the time of the Neanderthals.

After a long drive we found our base for the next four days, a quaint little bed-and-breakfast in the middle of large white fields. We settled into our room and as night fell our host Marc, who had been out in the field all day, welcomed us to the land of the White Ghost. We were exhausted and excited and ready for an early night and a quick start; after all we had already missed Day One because of the flight detour.

We rose at five the next morning, with breakfast at six. It was still dark when we sat down to eat a wonderful Canadian spread which we were soon struggling to cope with. Marc insisted we ate it all as we would be burning lots of calories once we got out into the field. The insistence of the early start had to do with the weather. If it looked as if the sky was clear, then we had to be in position before sunrise. If, instead, it was overcast then we could go back inside and have another coffee. As it happened it was sufficiently clear and we were soon putting on our third layer of clothing and our snow boots on the porch, collecting our cameras and tripods ready to go, while making sure we didn't slip on the ice.

The drive, still in the dark, was a short one but the subsequent 500-metre walk in the deep snow made us question our sanity. Marc told us to stop close to what appeared to be a small pile of boulders in an otherwise anonymous landscape of flat white. We were to set up here and it wasn't easy with so much clothing while out of breath. Still we struggled and set up our heavy cameras and lenses, all well protected against the low temperatures (a 'warm' −10°C). We had several spare batteries tucked away in the pockets of our base layers, where they would be kept warm by our body heat. Batteries last only a short time in low temperatures so you have to be well prepared for such a trip.

The dark blue of the early morning sky was gradually turning paler with hints of orange and pink merging when the White Ghost made its first appearance (Figure 5). Silent, as all owls are in flight, a spectacular snowy owl appeared out of nowhere to sit on the precise pile of rocks which lay in front of us. Too dark to take any pictures, we admired the beautiful animal, a star of Harry Potter movies, in its wild state. Snowy owls come down here from

Figure 5 The White Ghost.

the High Arctic in winter and they carve out the fields into territories with viewing platforms, like the rock pile, from where they can observe and hunt rodents. Coming down from the Arctic, where they would have had little contact with humans, the owl appeared oblivious to our presence as it got on with its task of spotting its next meal.

The next few days gave us ample opportunities to get up close to these magical birds and to observe their behaviour at close quarters. We could see why they are called White Ghosts. They would approach us with a low-level flight, almost touching the ground. Particularly during blizzards, we were hard pressed to see their approach until they were upon us. A poor unsuspecting rodent would have no chance against this formidable stealth predator.

There are some animals that leave a powerful impact on you when you see them close up. In this book we will meet several. The snowy owl is in that league. We thought of these birds outside our caves in Gibraltar and what the Neanderthals would have made of the arrival of something new, something they had not seen before in their lives, something white and ghost-like. We can only imagine.

Judging from records from sites across Western and Central Europe[1], snowy owls became a regular feature during the onset of the last Ice Age. This makes complete sense as we have seen that much of the region was taken over by steppe-tundra. As the Tundra was forced south from the High Arctic, which was engulfed by ice, the snowy owls were forced well south. Their world changed. Certainly the Tundra would have been much the same as in the north but in these mid-latitudes they had to adapt to a new day–night regime, quite different from the 24-hour summer days and 24-hour winter nights of the Arctic. Climate may change often and repeatedly but latitude and corresponding day–night regimes do not, and the Neanderthals, like the snowy owls, would have had to adapt their lifestyles depending not just on climate but also on latitude.

In winter, just like today, snowy owls would have moved south from the breeding grounds as they became inhospitable for a few months. Their southward movements would have taken them into the Iberian Peninsula, then not far away at all, and some reached all the way down to Gibraltar. They didn't get there because there was Tundra in Gibraltar—there wasn't, just as there isn't in Ontario today—but simply because conditions to the north forced them south. The degree of movement, like today, may well have been dependent on rodent availability. In a good rodent year, they may never have reached Gibraltar. Only when food was scarce further north would they have been pushed this far south. Neanderthals probably only saw snowy owls in Gibraltar in years when the rodent populations of southern France and northern Spain crashed, even though they did not know it.

Such events may seem unusual to us today but go back to North America and you'd be surprised. In 2014 a combination of extreme cold and a crash in the lemming population drove many snowy owls south from Canada well into the United States, with some birds being spotted as far south as Florida[2]; at 30°N, these birds had reached latitudes well south of Gibraltar (at 36°N). The conditions are not right today in Western Europe, with the warm Atlantic waters bathing its shores, and rare winter sightings of snowy owls in Britain and France cause a stir among birders. It was certainly very different during the onset of the last Ice Age.

These observations lead me to one conclusion. Neanderthals came across snowy owls at times, maybe frequently in some places, but this does not mean that the Neanderthals inhabited the Tundra as it is clear that snowy owls were being pushed south of the Tundra. At Gibraltar, Neanderthals certainly saw these birds, almost certainly on the coastal sand dunes just as they have recently been observed in Florida.

So Stewart's analysis of the birds which reached Gibraltar from the far north boils down to two main types: sea duck and Tundra predators. Of the latter, one was the snowy owl and a second the rough-legged buzzard. The birds of the Taiga kept to the forest belts which barely penetrated the Iberian Peninsula and they never reached the southerly latitude of Gibraltar.

Now here's the really interesting thing. As these birds came south we might have expected the Mediterranean birds to have moved further south and abandoned the Gibraltar area, either in response to changing conditions or to accommodate the new arrivals. The first reason, that they would have abandoned the area because of changing conditions, we have almost discarded already. After all, we have seen that snowy owls, long-tailed ducks, and others did not reach these latitudes following habitats and associated climates but rather because they were pushed south by conditions elsewhere. But would long-tailed ducks have pushed other kinds of duck further south? Would snowy owls have similarly displaced Mediterranean owls?

The answer is that they didn't. These birds came in but those already there never left and this created strange assemblages of species which have no equivalent anywhere today. As the ice advanced across north-western Europe, birds were pushed south but the ones in the south stayed put. Everything now occupying

Europe, from Gibraltar in the south to Varanger in the north, was compressed into Western and Central Europe and south to the shores of the Mediterranean. Something similar happened with the mammals, except that the Tundra species never reached the most southerly latitudes. The Neanderthals found themselves living in this zone of compression.

Can we establish what impact this progressive compression had on the Neanderthals? We can guess by comparing the mammals associated with Neanderthal sites with those associated with later Modern Human sites. Which species are more frequent in Neanderthal sites than in Modern Human sites? Among the herbivores there is a clear suite of species: red deer, aurochs, boar, giant deer, the temperate rhinos of the genus *Dicerorhinus* typical of savannah environments, and the Spanish ibex. The one exception seems to be the woolly rhinoceros, which we might have expected to have become more abundant as woodland receded at the expense of steppe-tundra. Overall, the species that appear to have gone into decline, probably remaining in warm southern refugia, are the species of warm temperate wooded environments. We see a similar picture when we look at the carnivores: spotted hyena, cave bear, wild cat, leopard, Spanish lynx, weasel, badger, and polecat. The Neanderthals were a part of this receding community of mammals.

In contrast, the species on the increase and associated with Modern Humans were those of open, generally treeless habitats which would have been largely steppe-tundra: reindeer, horse, chamois, woolly mammoth, ibex, musk ox, moose, Arctic fox, red fox, wolf, lynx, and wolverine. Lion and brown bear, large predators capable of surviving in a variety of circumstances, appear to have neither declined nor increased between Neanderthal and Modern Human sites.

All this points to a very clear picture which supports what the long-tailed ducks and snowy owls and other birds have already shown us: of a progressive expansion of the steppe-tundra across Europe, retention of the warm woodland fauna in the south, and the presence of communities of species which would otherwise not be found together.

CHAPTER 6

GIBRALTAR

In the following chapters we will try and establish what kind of relationship, if any, Neanderthals had with birds. Before we can do this we need to establish exactly which species they came into regular contact with and which habitats they regularly frequented, where they came across these birds. In the previous chapters I have tried to introduce the impact of climate change on Neanderthals through the movements of birds from the Arctic and boreal regions that they would not have normally encountered within their geographical range had it not been for the climate changes that affected Europe towards the height of the last Ice Age. Now it is time to find out which species they would have been familiar with on a regular basis.

Let me start with Gibraltar, with which I am most familiar but which also has the longest list of bird species for any Neanderthal site anywhere in the world: 160 species, which approximately equates to 30 per cent of the bird species found in Europe today. This is a massive number considering we are talking of bird remains found in four caves in a 6-kilometre-long limestone peninsula. So it is a good place to start.

Gibraltar has tall limestone cliffs which rise from sea level up to 426 metres at its highest peak. At the base of the peak, at sea level, lie Gorham's and Vanguard Caves, two of the main Neanderthal occupation sites which we have been excavating for close to thirty years (Figure 6, Plate 2). Examining the birds that shared this world with the Neanderthals, a group of species emerges which are striking because of the regularity with which they show up. Archaeological level after archaeological level of Neanderthal occupation produces the same species over and over again. These are no longer long-tailed ducks or snowy owls that show up from time to time. These are instead birds that would have been very much a part of the Neanderthal ecological context, in Gibraltar at least.

Birds which nest in cliffs and rocky outcrops are consistent in the cave record. This is not surprising given the large area of cliff habitat which would have been available to them. The most abundant birds, judging from the large number of bones found inside the caves, were choughs. Their presence in the caves spanned tens of thousands of years, matching that of the Neanderthals which

Figure 6 The Rock of Gibraltar with the Neanderthal caves at its base.

started during the last interglacial around 127 000 years ago and continued until around 32 000 years ago[1]. Choughs are corvids, members of the large crow family. They are unusual among corvids in having long, curved, beaks which are used for probing for invertebrates in soft earth. There are only two species in the world and they are characteristic of the rocky mountain belts that span from the Iberian Peninsula in the west to the Himalayas in the east.

Today one species, the red-billed chough, generally lives lower down the mountains than its cousin the yellow-billed (or Alpine) chough. Red-billed chough remains are the more frequent of the two species in the Gibraltar caves but yellow-billed choughs are not rare birds. It seems that, unlike today when the two species are largely isolated from each other by altitude, choughs at the time of the Neanderthals occurred side by side. This does not only apply to Gibraltar as there are many Neanderthal sites across Eurasia with both species of chough present.

It seems that the compression phenomenon which we have seen in the case of Arctic birds, where they were forced into contact with species from further south, may have also applied to mountain birds. It seems likely that as cold conditions set in the high mountains became inhospitable, forcing yellow-billed choughs down the mountains and into direct contact with the red-billed choughs. During milder periods the yellow-billed choughs returned up the mountains. This would explain why sometimes we find only red-billed choughs in Gibraltar and the two species at other times. The third alternative, of only yellow-billed choughs, which would be the case if the red-billed choughs had been displaced southwards, does not occur.

This is a neat story but there may be more to it than this. There are places in Morocco today where yellow-billed choughs come right down to the coast and it is possible to observe both species feeding side by side. Admittedly this is not a widespread occurrence but it leaves the door open to interpreting why it is that both species were frequent neighbours across wide areas of their range at the time of the Neanderthals and now they are not. It serves to illustrate how much care we have to take when interpreting the past on the basis of our knowledge of the present.

Cambridge zoologist Nathan Emery has defined corvids as 'feathered apes'[2] on account of their remarkable intelligence, unparalleled in the bird world. Corvids were among the birds that were ever-present in Neanderthal contexts. To the choughs we can add ravens and jackdaws in particular and these are, like the choughs, birds of rocky habitats. Over and over again, Neanderthals occupying caves and rock shelters along cliff lines as at Gibraltar would have lived in the permanent presence of these noisy, social, and highly intelligent birds. These are birds that would have been bold enough to come close to the cave entrances or followed the Neanderthals to pick scraps from the remains of their hunts.

I have spent many hours in photographic hides which have been baited with carcasses close by in order to attract vultures. Almost invariably the first birds to arrive at the carrion have been ravens, carrion crows, magpies, and azure-winged magpies; the latter three species tend to nest on trees rather than cliffs but they also appear alongside the troglodyte corvids in many Neanderthal sites. They arrive almost as soon as the meat has been laid out and the coast is clear, a matter of minutes at most. As the corvids arrive at the food which has been laid out for the vultures they enter a kind of frenzied activity, hurriedly and noisily picking off tiny morsels, but they need the large vultures to come in and open up the carcasses so I suspect that a lot of the noise and aerial activity is designed to draw the vultures' attention to the location of the food. Soon the vultures arrive.

All this would have been known to the Neanderthals who would have used the intelligent corvids in the same way as the vultures, as an early warning system of the presence of a nearby kill. This, in itself, is a sign of cognitive capacity. It would then have been up to the Neanderthals to get in first ahead of all the other observers of corvid behaviour—hyenas, wolves, and vultures included.

Ravens and carrion crows in particular are also of use to vultures and other birds by announcing the arrival of a large and dangerous predator such as the golden eagle. These powerful eagles will readily dive at the large vultures to chase them away from their territories and are perfectly capable of inflicting serious damage on their victims, occasionally even killing them. To the vultures the persistent calls of ravens over the horizon, mobbing a golden eagle, is a signal to quickly get out of the way. For a Neanderthal, unthreatened by the eagle, it may have had other connotations, as we will see in Chapter 17. For now, we can stay with the idea that ravens and golden eagles went together hand-in-hand as part of the aerial displays and battles which they observed daily in the skies above their homes.

I have observed the different rock-dwelling corvids and raptors that once inhabited Gibraltar's cliffs on many occasions and in different situations. Most have been in the high mountains, in places like the Pyrenees, which is where these species still survive well away from human activity. When I then return home and visit the Neanderthal caves once again, looking up at the verticality of the sheer cliffs that appear to continue endlessly upwards until they clash with the blue sky, I transpose the images from the mountains which have been imprinted in my mind. The fossils from the caves come to life once again in the skies above the Rock of Gibraltar.

Something that I am unable to reproduce anywhere, not even in my mind, is the sheer quantity of animals which would have inhabited the cliffs and plains surrounding Gibraltar at the time of the Neanderthals. We do not seem to realize how impoverished the world we live in has become. It's not just the endangered species or those on the brink of extinction, it's actually a lot worse. Judging from the numbers of remains of birds and other animals in the caves the decline from the Pleistocene to today has been catastrophic beyond belief. Even a comparison with accounts by naturalists over the past two hundred years is sufficient to make us realize the extent of the ecological tragedy. If a Neanderthal, by some miracle, woke up and saw the world we live in he or she would struggle to understand why the skies are so empty and would weep with sorrow. It was so different back then. Their world, which took hundreds of millennia to shape, has been destroyed by civilized Man in a few centuries[3]. This is an important point that we must keep well in mind when we come to discuss Neanderthal abilities, in particular the catching of birds.

I recall my first time in England, as a keen eleven-year old bird watcher (as we were called then—for reasons beyond my understanding, it seems that for some time now the term birder has been preferred), looking up at what seemed empty skies. Having been brought up with the natural instinct of automatically looking up every time I came out of the house, and expecting to see specks in the sky, the situation was not only odd, it brought my spirits down. I was used to seeing hundreds, even thousands, of raptors overhead as they migrated between Europe and Africa. This was a daily occurrence in spring and autumn when we got the westerly winds. Here, in England in the 1960s, there wasn't a single raptor to be seen.

Even worse, people were obviously not used to raptors in the skies and didn't expect to see them. This was the time when ospreys were beginning to return as breeding birds to Scotland, in places like Loch Garten in the Scottish Highlands. I remember being taken to see the ospreys there but they had not bred that year so I missed them. Seeing an osprey was a big deal in Britain then but I knew them well from Gibraltar. A few days later I was on the Firth of Forth looking for waders[4]. There were plenty of other bird watchers there too, all staring down their telescopes at the birds feeding in the mud. To my excitement an osprey, on migration, flew right over me and the others. Nobody else saw it.

For the Neanderthals, looking up at the skies above Gibraltar would have presented views that would even overwhelm me. There wouldn't have just been the migrants, like today, but also those nesting and roosting on the cliffs. Corvids apart, the cliffs of Gibraltar were home to golden eagles, Bonelli's eagles, white-tailed eagles, bearded vultures, griffon vultures, Egyptian vultures, peregrine falcons, Eleonora's falcons, kestrels, and lesser kestrels. To the already crowded skies we would add tree-nesting raptors from the coastal plains: cinereous vulture, booted eagle, red kite, black kite, common buzzard, and, in all probability, Spanish imperial eagle[5]. Big birds of prey in the sky were part of the daily lives of the Gibraltar Neanderthals as they would have been in many sites across their range. This is important and will be worth recalling when we get to discuss the relationships between Neanderthals and birds.

I have made reference to tree-nesting raptors that occupied the coastal plains. These plains, which extended several kilometres outside the caves at the time of the Neanderthals were drowned by sea level rise[6] with global warming 10 000 years ago. We know from deposits inside the caves that the plains were sandy with mobile dunes. In one location, where the dunes encountered the cliffs of Gibraltar, the wind forced them upwards, defying gravity. Today we can see this ancient dune, now fossilized, as an impressive feature reaching 300 metres above sea level. Pollen and fossil charcoal found inside the caves has given us a good idea of the plants which grew on this coastal plain, the hunting ground of the Neanderthals, but it was the birds that enabled us to recreate the most detailed picture of this ancient Neanderthal landscape.

The work was done by my wife Geraldine as part of her doctoral thesis[7]. It was another way in which birds helped us understand the world of the Neanderthals. To do this she worked with the species of birds whose remains had been found inside the caves at the time of the Neanderthals. She concentrated on those species which occupied vegetated habitats of some sort. What she did was elegant.

For several years Geraldine travelled the length and breadth of the Iberian Peninsula. I accompanied her whenever possible and acted as her field assistant. Our son Stewart, then a young ten-year old, came along too and began to learn his trade at this early age. The plan was neat and simple. Geraldine placed 100×100-kilometre grids on maps for the area which she intended to visit and subdivided these into smaller 10×10-kilometre units which were given identifying codes. Then, using a random number generator, she picked particular squares at random for sampling. In the years of her fieldwork she sampled over 1000 such points, always 1-hectare plots within the selected 10×10-kilometre squares. These were spread across the range of climates and habitats available in the Iberian Peninsula today.

In each square, Geraldine painstakingly mapped out the habitat structure, which is how plants, rocks, or any other objects were arranged within the plot. So she measured such things as tree, shrub, and grass height, tree density, or amount of open, bare ground. In parallel all the bird species identified within each plot were recorded. The net result was that for each species of bird recorded across the Iberian Peninsula, Geraldine could amalgamate the results from all the plots where each species had been identified and reconstruct a detailed picture of the habitat structure that each bird species required.

She was now in the position of being able to examine which birds were found in each Neanderthal archaeological horizon and, using her present-day data, pool the results for all the species found. Armed with that powerful information she could then characterize, with numbers, the habitat structure on the coastal shelf outside the caves which is where the birds, and the Neanderthals, would have roamed.

CHAPTER 7

THE DYNAMIC WORLD
OF DUNES

The habitats of the ancient coastal shelf off Gibraltar, where the Neanderthals did most of their hunting and gathering, would have exposed them to a wide diversity of bird species. If we are to understand how and when Neanderthals interacted with birds we must be aware of what was available to them and what they would have come across. It is also important to see what the environment in which those exchanges took place would have been like, as it might offer clues as to what may have been possible and what may not.

So Geraldine's detailed analysis is an excellent start. What she found was that the habitats of the coastal shelf varied little through time. There was a remarkable constancy in spite of the severe climate changes which were affecting much of Europe at that time. This means that Neanderthals living in Gibraltar would have seen the world outside the cave as familiar and predictable. Seasonal changes in flowering, seed and fruit production, the timing of the deer rut, of the monk seal calving, the nesting, migration, and wintering of birds, and the filling and drying out of lakes and ponds would all have followed a regular annual pattern. Neanderthal children would have learnt the ways of their parents, who would themselves have learnt them from their parents. Success in survival in this world was aided by cultural transmission.

This is in direct contrast with what was happening to other Neanderthals living on the edge of their world, where gigantic woolly creatures with long trunks were encroaching into their territory, which was fast shrinking at the expense of frozen ground in which little could grow. The changes would have been toing and froing as climate cooled and warmed in a world of uncertainty[1]. The skills of the grandparents, who had lived in traditional woodland settings, might have been rendered obsolete by the time the grandchildren were running around in places where it was hard to find a tree and recognize it for what it was. And their grandchildren, in turn, might not have known what trees were when eventually these came back during a brief spell of warmth.

One question which archaeologists often debate is why the way in which Neanderthals made stone tools was so similar over thousands of years, contrasting with the apparent diversity in tool making by Modern Humans. The attribution of tool technologies to Modern Humans at the time when they entered Europe is something that worries me because I am not convinced that the supporting evidence is really that robust. But let's leave that to one side for now, because what I want to do is contrast how people would have behaved in worlds that they perceived as constant and in those that they saw as highly unpredictable. Unpredictability has been our nemesis throughout our history and it still consumes us today in our everyday lives, be it forecasting weather or financial markets. It would have been the same for the Neanderthals, worrying about when it might be hot enough for the red deer to come to the waterholes to drink so as to wait for them in ambush or watching the displays of the golden eagles for signs of the arrival of spring weather. Getting it right has always been of vital importance to us, and getting it wrong has been a pivotal force in evolution.

Coming back to constancy in tool making, if the Neanderthals over millennia had developed tools which were ideally suited to the animals they hunted and plants which they collected in particular environments, why change? Is this constancy really a sign of ineptitude? On the other hand, all the technological novelty, incidentally some of which is thought to have been Neanderthal innovation[2], that we observe from around 40 000 years ago in Europe occurs in areas which are under the constant shadow of the encroaching ice world. It is very likely that technological diversity reflected attempts at ways of dealing with a new world, one of ice, tundra, and the large herds of herbivores that went with it.

In Gibraltar, Neanderthals experienced the climatic and ecological constancy that they had known for millennia right until the very end. They never changed their ways but, then again, they never had the need to do so. When change came it was so sharp and rapid and so few Neanderthals were left that there was no time for adaptation, only extinction.

The predictable world of the Gibraltar Neanderthals starts off with a heterogeneous landscape of woodland, thickets, grassy meadows, seasonal lakes, and rocky and sandy coasts, backed by the steep cliffs which I described in Chapter 6. Its heterogeneity was maintained by the action of the wind on the dunes. The Strait of Gibraltar, a narrow channel of the sea linking the Atlantic Ocean with the Mediterranean Sea, is famous for its winds. The high mountains on the southern (Rif Mountains in North Africa) and northern (Betic Mountains in Southern Europe) shores exacerbate the situation by acting as a funnel. The prevailing winds follow the orientation of the Strait, which is east to west.

The fossil sand dune on Gibraltar's eastern flank, which I described in Chapter 6, is an example of how ancient winds piled up the sand. Go 60 and 180 metres up the Rock, somewhere above Gorham's Cave, and you find other dunes, once formed at sea level and forced up and fossilized by the tectonic uplift of the Rock as African and Eurasian plates collided here. Perhaps the best illustration of the speed of dune movement, and the best classroom that I had to help me understand dune dynamics, was in the Doñana National Park in south-western Spain.

This was one of Geraldine's study areas and we often regard it as a good proxy for the ancient coastal dune habitats which once existed off Gibraltar. Here in Doñana, the dunes moved at impressive rates and the stone pine trees, ideally suited for colonizing the dunes as they have a short generation time, were in a constant life-and-death struggle. The dunes would move rapidly inland and surround copses of pine trees, known by the locals as 'corrales'. The corral spelt the death of that particular group of pine trees. Like a group of Neanderthals isolated and surrounded by inhospitable conditions, the pines were progressively incorporated into a growing dune until only the needles on the crowns or the tallest trees remained visible. In time they would also drown and we wouldn't know that trees had once grown there.

The best example of dune speed came during one of our visits. We slammed the brakes on in our 4×4 as a tall brick structure appeared right in front of us in the middle of the dunes. Here, where the countryside was so desert-like that filmmakers had once chosen it to film parts of *Lawrence of Arabia*, was a strange structure looming upwards perhaps 20 or more metres into the blue sky. In time, and after talking to the local wardens, we realized that the structure was a defunct well (Figure 7). It had been dug into the dune to reach the water table. Then the dune moved and left

Figure 7 The old well at Doñana. As the dunes moved on the well was exposed and left 'hanging' in the air.

the well hanging in mid-air. Judging from the apparent age of the structure all this would have happened in under a century.

So the moving dunes at Gibraltar would have ensured that the landscape was heterogeneous. Pine woods came and went. As the dunes became stabilized away from the coast junipers would have taken hold. In time the cork oak trees and the olives, the latter probably dispersing from the limestone Rock itself, would have established themselves. Paradoxically, this constantly changing world gave the Neanderthals predictability. In one sense it was certainly changing but, in another, the landscape always had dunes, pine woods, and all the rest. The wind simply changed their location.

One of the most relaxing experiences that makes me feel at home and within my comfort zone is sitting under the shade of a cork oak tree on a warm early spring morning. These trees are often scattered across the landscape in a kind of open parkland, reminiscent of a savannah. Birds are singing everywhere, the open fields and shrubs under the trees are covered in flowers and, occasionally, a red deer cautiously emerges and stealthily moves along. The scene has not changed much since the days of the Neanderthals and the birds are the same ones.

These southern European savannahs are habitats for the spring and many birds arrive here from Africa to make the most of the insect abundance generated by the heat and the diversity of flowering plants. By early summer many have departed in order to avoid the long, hot, and dry summer when temperatures soar above 40°C and there is no rain for at least three months. The autumn sees the passage of migrants on the way south towards Africa and, later on, the arrival of others that will remain for the winter. The climate is milder on the coast than inland, where temperatures drop below zero regularly, especially in January and February. If Neanderthals sought food in these habitats, then my guess is that it would not have been in the summer but, instead during the wet months from October to early June. At other times of the year they would have moved to other habitats and, if they were close by, up into high mountains as these opened up in the summer.

One of the attractions of this habitat to birds is the holes within the trunks of the larger trees which are ideal for nesting. Some are natural but many others have been drilled by woodpeckers. At Gibraltar, as in most sites today, the Iberian green woodpecker and the great spotted woodpecker were the culprits. The Neanderthals would have been familiar with these large and colourful birds and their sounds. The green woodpecker emits a distinctive loud shriek as it flies, and the great spotted woodpecker's resonating drumming as it drills into the wood is one of the defining sounds of these woods. These calls along with the persistent 'upupu-upupu' of the hoopoe, the incessant song of the chaffinch, and the varied mix of the great mimic of all sounds and noises, the spotless starling, would have been the sounds of the Neanderthal woods, bringing seasonal familiarity along with the colours and scents of the spring.

It is quite remarkable how many of the species[3] which characterize this habitat have been found inside the Gibraltar caves, even though this habitat no longer exists outside the caves, because the coastal shelf in which it was located was submerged around 10 000 years ago. The list of species reveals the richness of the habitat, and we'll explore this later, when we look into the quality of different habitats occupied by Neanderthals. The coincidence in species between today and the time of the Neanderthals is amazing, particularly when we consider how climatically different the world was then from now. It really is a tribute to the resilience of these habitats in the low latitudes of Europe. They are the ecological basis of a glacial refuge.

CHAPTER 8

LAKES AND PLAINS

The coastal shelf where all this habitat was situated has been submerged for 10 000 years[1]. This has not deterred Geraldine and for a number of years she and other members of the Gibraltar Museum's Underwater Research Unit (URU), along with colleagues from the United Kingdom headed by Geoff Bailey at the University of York and Nic Flemming at the University of Southampton, have been diving the waters off Gorham's Cave in search of clues about this submerged landscape. This is really tough work. I have been on the diving boats and seen for myself the difficulty of undertaking underwater archaeological surveys and excavations. Everything needs that much more planning than on land and field time is heavily constrained, particularly when diving deep.

So far no Neanderthals have been found on the sea bed but one result really spurs the imagination. At some 30 metres depth, somewhere off Gorham's Cave, there are pinnacles of a sedimentary rock[2] which is quite different from the limestone of the Rock itself. Some of the stone tools made by Neanderthals and found inside the cave appear to have been made from pebbles of precisely this kind of rock. Limestone, though abundant, is not easy to shape into tools as it shatters easily. Neanderthals sought flint and other suitable rocks for their tools and the pinnacles seem to have been a likely source which was not too far away.

The most exciting aspect of the pinnacles is the result of the contact of the Gibraltar limestone with rocks that make up the pinnacles and which continue out to sea as part of the sea bed. All the water that falls on Gibraltar drains through the porous limestone, forming caves in the process, and works its way underground towards the sea. When it reaches the impermeable rocks by the pinnacles it comes to the surface and Geraldine could dive down there and see the freshwater coming to the surface even now. Imagine a time when all this was the surface, the pressure of the sea above was removed, and water came up to form lakes and ponds. Now we could understand the presence of another group of birds inside the Neanderthal caves.

There are lots of bones of amphibians—frogs, toads, and newts—inside the caves. These indicate that freshwater must have been present at some time of the year if such animals were to survive. Sometimes the preservation was so good inside the caves that we found the remains of ancient ponds, with caked mud formed as they had dried, and of the tiny frogs that had made the most of the seasonal water. These conditions would have been replicated in many places outside the caves but the evidence would have been long gone. It was the presence of aquatic birds that suggested to us that some of these water bodies were larger than tiny ponds.

Today, in the dune world of Doñana, we find lakes of all shapes and sizes where the water table reaches the surface and dunes act as barriers keeping the water from escaping towards the sea. They fill during the wet season and gradually dry in the summer. Only the larger, deeper, lakes retain some water all year. Most are dry in the summer. These lakes are usually surrounded by pine savannahs so the birds of that habitat, the species I listed in Chapter 7, have easy access to freshwater. Others would have come in especially for the water like they do today and, once again, the match between Neanderthal times and today is astonishing. There were ducks of many species[3]. Some of these species have broad climatic tolerance but red-crested pochard and marbled teal are species of warm climates contrasting with the long-tailed duck, scoters, and eider which we have already seen would have come down from the north in winter. This indicates the kind of packing of species of different backgrounds which we would find strange today, the result of the pushing south of northern species without an equivalent shift of those already in these latitudes. The image of a flock of long-tailed ducks resting on a coastal lagoon along-side a group of red-crested pochards is one that would bewilder any ornithologist today.

Duck are not the only wetland species to appear in the Neanderthal levels. There are species which are still found in these habitats today and indicative of mild climatic conditions[4]. The herons, ibises, and crakes are birds of rank aquatic vegeta-tion, typical of swamps. The purple heron is a species of warm cli-mates, arriving in the spring from tropical Africa and leaving with the onset of the summer drought. The collared pratincole, also a spring arrival from tropical Africa, would make the most of the drying mud pans where it would lay its eggs on the ground, a dan-gerous enterprise. These birds nest in large colonies which gives them some degree of protection from ground predators. Would the Neanderthals have ventured into the colonies to collect their eggs? This is something we may never know, as egg shells would be hard to find preserved. What we can say is that Neanderthals would have had no difficulty, nor needed any technology, to raid a colony of collared pratincoles. All they would have needed was a knowledge of where and when to search, a memory from years past and a keen eye to spot the cryptic eggs, and they would have left no trace of their actions for archaeologists to find. In other words, the cognitive skills of an intelligent human.

The spotted crake and the black-winged stilt are typically summer visitors to Europe from tropical Africa today but the climatic conditions of the extreme south-west of the Iberian Peninsula allow some to remain all winter, a unique situation in Europe. Did they overwinter also at the time of the Neanderthals? Other species provide the climate contrast we have observed with the ducks. The red-throated diver is a bird that breeds on Arctic lakes and migrates south as far as the British Isles in the winter. Some stray south into the Iberian Peninsula today but they are quite scarce. In winter they move to the coast, staying offshore or on coastal lagoons, behaving just like the sea duck. Their presence in Neanderthal levels suggests that they were also caught up in the ice-generated southward shift of species' ranges.

The coastal lakes would have been surrounded by swampy ground and wet meadows. It is here that many species would have hunted. The white storks or the black kites, which nested on the trees in the pine savannahs, would have had a short flight to habitats rich in reptiles, amphibians, and small mammals. The swampy ground would have been teeming with life and would have provided plenty of cover for any Neanderthal prepared to wade. Among the reeds and bulrushes they would have found the floating nests of many aquatic birds so, again, the eggs of coots, crakes, stilts, and terns would have been hard to find, requiring mental skills and memory from previous years, but easy to collect once located. The signal of this activity would remain archaeologically invisible.

The arrival of wintering species would have provided alternative food sources so long as they could be caught. We have no knowledge of what technology Neanderthals might have had at their disposal. Did they have nets or traps? Unfortunately, the materials from which such objects would have been made would have perished easily, leaving us, once more, with the absence of evidence conundrum. One thing we do know is that Neanderthals were skilled ambush hunters. This alone shows that they had an intimate knowledge of their surroundings and the behaviour of the animals which they hunted. Planning, a hallmark of Mellars' modernity, would have been essential. That they despatched deer and other herbivores by ambushing them and using thrusting spears is not in question. So why not use a similar technique to hunt birds?

Which birds would these be? They would have to be large enough to make the effort worthwhile. Ducks might be an option and certainly large numbers would flock in the winter. Another group arrived in the winter and these would have covered the wet fields as they grazed. In Doñana, greylag geese arrive from Denmark in huge numbers in the winter today, up to 80 000 in some years. They don't just graze in the fields.

Every morning in the winter, while dark, the sound of thousands of honking geese dominates these marshes. What are these birds doing so early? Nobody is really certain but what they do is fly to the dunes where they will land and spend the early minutes of the new day clustered among the dunes in large numbers. It is thought that they go there to ingest sand which will aid them in their digestion. After all, not many birds are strict vegetarians like the geese and grit in the stomach is a good substitute for teeth. The geese seem to be especially fond of particular dunes and it is easy for an intelligent hunter to plan to go to these ahead of them in the dark and lie in wait.

We haven't found the remains of greylags in our caves so far but we do have those of other geese. These are of species which are rare this far south today. They belong to barnacle and brent geese. These are birds which breed in the Arctic. I recall a wonderful experience on the beautiful but cold island of Islay in the Inner Hebrides one January. Here we went to see the spectacle of the barnacle geese and found no fewer than 40 000 of these birds spread right across the island. They fed in the fields and noisily rose into the skies whenever something disturbed them, creating a magical scene of thousands of airborne geese. These birds come from eastern Greenland, performing a spectacular migration across the North Atlantic with a staging post on Iceland before arriving in Ireland and western Scotland. Of course, at the time of the Neanderthals these areas were under ice so they too were forced southwards all the way down to Gibraltar.

Another January we were on the Cley marshes in Norfolk. Here the geese in the fields were brent geese. These birds had come from another direction, this time from Russian Siberia, west of the Taymyr Peninsula. Their migration, a journey of around 4500 kilometres, is twice that of the Greenland barnacle geese although large ocean crossings are not required. These geese fly west along the Arctic coasts of Russia towards the White Sea (some 600 kilometres south-east of Varanger) and then overland towards the Gulfs of Finland and Bothnia, crossing the Baltic, Denmark, and northern Germany to reach their winter quarters in the Netherlands, western France, and south-east England. Once again the entire route would have been closed to brent geese during the build up to the last Ice Age. Barnacle and brent geese therefore fit into the same pattern as the long-tailed duck. It is as a result of southward forcing by ice that Neanderthals came across these geese in Gibraltar. Whether they amassed in the numbers we saw on Islay and Cley we will never know. Perhaps, Neanderthals hid in the dunes off Gorham's Cave and anticipated the excitement of the dawn ambush when they heard the flight calls of the geese.

The richness of the fields surrounding the lakes, between these and the pine savannahs, included two large species that had the potential of being ambush hunted with the hope of, given their size, a great return. These were the great and little bustards, both of which appear among the other birds in the Gibraltar caves. Great bustards would have been among the largest birds that Neanderthals would have come across anywhere in their range. The large males may weigh up to 18 kilos and the smaller females may exceed 5 kilos. The little bustards are, as the name suggests, smaller with males around the 1-kilo mark and females just over 0.5 kilos.

Bustards like open fields without trees and they are notoriously difficult to approach, at least in today's world. In East Africa, I have found the Kori bustard remarkably approachable so we simply don't know if the European bustards' wariness is part of their way or simply the product of millennia of persecution. To observe great and little bustards at close quarters we have always had to arrive before first light, and very quietly. Once inside our hide we have found that the birds come very close, oblivious of our presence, sometimes so close that we couldn't fit them into the frame with our telephoto lenses. So, again, a stealthy and clever ambush hunter can potentially get very close to bustards.

The bustards raise another important aspect that could have a bearing on Neanderthal ambush hunting behaviour. These birds lek. That is, the males defend territories in the spring where they display to try to attract females. Flocks of females gather at these leks to watch the displaying males and choose the father of their next brood. An intelligent human would be able to observe, remember, and plan ambush visits to such leks. During these lekking performances, which always happen at first light, the males become so distracted with their performance that they can easily miss the approach of a ground predator. Did Neanderthals stalk lekking bustards?

The nineteenth-century naturalist Willoughby Verner described the beauty of colour and sounds of the grassy plains close to Gibraltar. Although much of it has been destroyed there are places where we can still enjoy this beauty. The great bustard was wiped out from this area barely a decade ago and little bustards are all but gone too. The smaller birds remain, even though their numbers are declining rapidly as a result of agriculture. The species typical of these habitats are also found inside our caves[5]. Some of these birds would have been breeding in the fields while others, like the northern wheatear, would have been on passage.

The northern wheatear is a species that breeds right across Europe, only on high mountains in the south, and reaches up to Greenland, north-eastern Canada, and Alaska. All these birds winter in tropical Africa, so for a bird that only weighs around 24 grams (10 grams more in the case of the Greenland race) this is a remarkable journey. The Alaskan birds spend the winter in East Africa and twice a year make a journey of 14 600 kilometres between breeding and wintering grounds. This species is one that would have thrived in glacial Europe. Even though much of its habitat in Greenland and northern Europe would have been under ice, the steppe-tundra that spread across Europe would have made it a paradise for this species that would have opportunistically come in for the summer months, leaving back to Africa in the autumn. Neanderthals in Gibraltar would have seen the northern wheatears on the move just as we have regularly seen them on the coastal dunes of Doñana in the autumn migration, loving the soft sand where they can pick up beetles and other insects as part of their refuelling stop-over ahead of the crossing of the Sahara. The Neanderthals would not have known the journey the birds undertook but their arrival at particular times of the year would have been a seasonal marker. The recognition of such seasonal markers is another measure of cognitive capacities.

CHAPTER 9

THE GREAT AUK

'It has arrived, it has arrived!' is the exclamation that I hear as Stewart comes into my office. I know exactly what he means so I don't waste a second and rush downstairs with Geraldine, who had heard the commotion. In the garden of the museum, placed on the lawn, was a large wooden box. It wasn't as large as Nana and Flint's box (Chapter 1) but it was still quite big. It was time to open it carefully with screwdrivers and gentle touches from a hammer on a screwdriver wedged between the wooden slats. The excitement was palpable but we had to move with care. Soon the top board was lifted only to reveal a mass of bubble wrap and tape. This was going to take a while.

Eventually the package was brought out of the box and the padding removed to reveal, in its full splendour, the best replica that I have ever seen of a great auk (*Pinguinus impennis*). Of all the birds recovered from Gorham's Cave there was only one species that we knew we couldn't ever hope to see or photograph alive today and this was it. Here we had the next best thing, a wonderful reproduction that would grace our museum (Figure 8).

Great auks were large, flightless seabirds which paid the price for losing their ability to fly. Like the Neanderthals, they had perceived their environment—the sea, and rocky predator-free islands where they could breed, fish, and escape marine predators

Figure 8 The sculpture of the great auk at the Gibraltar Museum.

by swimming fast—as stable in the long run. And so it had been for tens of millennia. So they invested in the ergonomic model that penguins had also invested in on the other side of the planet. They became flightless as a result but it posed no problem. Like the Neanderthals meeting the sudden loss of their wooded world, the great auk suddenly met a sharp environmental perturbation and by the year 1852 or shortly after it was extinct[1]. The perturbation was Man, arriving at the breeding colonies where the innocent creatures were clubbed to death by the thousands until none were left.

The great auk is generally considered to have lived in the North Atlantic, from Canada right across to the British Isles, but nobody is really sure how far south they bred. We find their remains inside the Neanderthal caves in Gibraltar and they ventured into the Mediterranean where they were painted on the walls of Cosquer Cave in southern France[2]. Were these birds wintering in the Mediterranean, swimming south each autumn just as penguins swim their way across the southern oceans today? Perhaps this was the case but I doubt it, especially if we place the appearance of this bird this far south in the context of what we have already seen with sea duck, divers, geese, and snowy owls.

I suspect that the presence of great auks this far south was part of the overall compression of species as a result of habitat loss in the north. In fact many of the historical island haunts of the great auk in Canada, Iceland, and the British Isles would have been covered by ice and so these birds had to have moved south, at least into the Bay of Biscay and adjacent areas. From here they would have moved further south during the winter. I am not convinced that these birds were only present in the winter, because in winter the birds would have stayed out at sea, just like other members of the auk family do today. That would have made the chances of their bones getting to the caves poor. So they must have been coming to land to breed on cliff ledges and crevices.

Something that really got Stewart and me thinking about the great auks and the possibility that they were actually nesting on Gibraltar was the diversity of seabird bones which were turning up inside the caves. They weren't all at sea level either. At Ibex Cave, a Neanderthal hunting station nearly 300 metres up the Rock on its eastern side, we found a well-preserved skull of a northern gannet. What was this gannet doing so high up on the cliffs?

On a cool but windless morning Geraldine and I drove into the small Scottish port town of Dunbar, close to the English border, facing the North Sea. As we parked we looked in the harbour among the scattering of fishing boats. A small group of people wearing Barbour jackets and with binoculars, tripods, and cameras showing inadvertently marked our fishing boat. Soon we introduced ourselves to our guides and fellow naturalists, and, after a briefing about the dos and don'ts aboard, we carefully descended some slippery-looking granite steps and jumped aboard. The fishing boat, rust showing in places, seemed seaworthy enough and we were happy that the sea was quiet even as we left the harbour and went round the first bluff and into the North Sea.

We sailed north for an hour, the dunes along the coast showing and keeping us comfortable in the knowledge that we were never too far from land. The first part of the journey was slow but soon enough we were entertained by small groups of puffins and guillemots flying past us, low over the water and beating their wings with great energy. If only their cousin the great auk had retained these powers we might still have them around today but, alas, the lure of increasing in size proved its downfall.

As we got closer to our target, northern gannets became increasingly frequent. Then, in the distance ahead of us we could see a small rocky island rising from the North Sea, right at the entrance to the Firth of Forth. As we got closer its height began to impress, as did the increasing number of gannets. A look through binoculars alerted us to the treat ahead. This was the Bass Rock, a 100-metre-high island just 2 kilometres offshore and boasting the largest gannet colony in the world, with around 150 000 birds at the peak of the breeding season.

We were now very close to the island when the boat's engines stopped and the crew prepared for what was to be one of nature's great spectacles. We prepared our cameras but weren't ready for what was to unfold. The gannets were soon over us along with many herring gulls and they obviously knew what was coming. Soon the crew started throwing fish overboard and every gannet in the sky started diving right in front of us, barely 5 metres away. The herring gulls tried to get in on the act but the aggressive gannets left little hope of success. Until then I had thought of herring gulls as aggressive birds but now I realized the connotations of the word gannet as kilos of fish were despatched in no time. The spectacle lasted for perhaps twenty minutes but the memory will last forever.

Scene One over, we now had the next part ahead of us. We had permission to land on the island and we were escorted by a warden from the Scottish Seabird Centre. The boat approached some steps close to a platform on the rocks of the island, tied up, and we quickly disembarked. This is the most problematic part of the visit. One out of three visits abort because of the state of the sea. Today we were lucky and we had four hours in which to explore the island and get in among the gannets. The strangest part of the briefing was the advice given to us about carrying a plastic A4 size card that was provided. I have to say we were so excited about visiting the island that we didn't really understand what the card was for. We found out the hard way that it was for our own protection.

The first thing that hits you when you land on the Bass Rock is not the noise of the gannets but the smell. It is an overpowering array of fish-related scents, stenches, and aromas that are beyond description. Imagine 75 000 occupied sites on the rock itself, each representing a pair and their chicks. Imagine what they produce each day, which stays by the nest, and imagine a hot day after a spell without rain. That is how we found the Bass Rock that late spring day.

You follow a prescribed path and soon gannets are staring at you in the eye. They don't seem to mind at all, being wholly preoccupied in themselves, their young, and their neighbours.

Photographing them is easy and you don't really need a long lens. The path eventually takes you to a flat area at the top where you can appreciate the full extent of the colony. Every bit of space is taken up and, as you make the final ascent, you pass so close to the sitting gannets that you cannot avoid brushing past them. They certainly have no intention of getting out of the way and that is why we needed the cards.

As you walk past they peck at your legs with their dagger-like beaks and it hurts. When we left the Bass Rock the photographs we had taken were not the only souvenirs. Our legs were badly bruised and scarred, bleeding from the constant attacks of the gannets sitting on their nests. If you hold the plastic cards beside your lower legs as you run the gauntlet then the gannets peck at these and you get by relatively unscathed. Getting past the gannets, trying desperately hard to avoid them, reminded us of the archaeologists who proclaimed that Neanderthals had been incapable of catching birds which were defined as fast-moving prey that would outrun (or outfly) the cumbersome Neanderthals. Not only were the Neanderthals agile, they were also clever enough to plan a seasonal cycle of activities relying on a deep knowledge of animal movements. Every student of the Neanderthals should do a little bit of natural history before making such unrealistic pronouncements. More examples will follow.

Aggression is the rule in a gannetry. Neighbours constantly attack each other violently. The scars from their combats are evident, particularly around the face. Gannets have no qualms about gouging out a neighbour's eye given the chance. The combination of white birds against dark rocks, the smell, and the noise, together with what can only be described as an inconclusive war of attrition among the players, could easily be the stuff of nightmares.

Yet, one cannot but come away with a sense of awe at having been a direct participant in one of nature's great spectacles.

Gannets reach Gibraltar today, particularly in the winter months, so it is possible that their remains in the Neanderthal caves were of such wintering birds. The problem, as with the great auk, is that the birds then are offshore and do not come to land at all. We would have to postulate a predator, perhaps the Neanderthal, going out to sea to catch them or scavenging carcasses along the beach. It seems that a lot of birds would have had to have been taken this way. And then again, this could apply to Gorham's Cave which was at a low level, but why take a gannet 300 metres up the Rock? Having been to the Bass Rock I am convinced that those ancient gannets were nesting on the cliffs of Gibraltar at a time when the Bass Rock and many other colonies in the North Sea and North Atlantic were closed for business because of the ice. If I am right then gannetries in Gibraltar would be part of the same phenomenon that drove sea duck, snowy owls, and geese down to the shores of the Strait of Gibraltar and the Mediterranean. My hunch is reinforced by the remains of many other North Atlantic seabirds in the caves[3]. You can find a similar assemblage today in the North Sea, with exceptions which are of great interest.

The main exception is the little auk which today nests much further north than the British Isles, on Svalbard and Greenland. Once more we have further evidence of the ice closing up the Arctic world and pushing birds south well beyond their present limits. With the seabirds too we see evidence of compression. The Mediterranean-breeding seabirds never left but had to absorb the contingents from the north. Mediterranean-breeding seabirds like the Balearic shearwater, Cory's shearwater, or the storm petrel squeezed in among the puffins and the gannets in the world of the Neanderthals.

For a number of years we have travelled to north-eastern England in June. North of Newcastle you reach the small coastal town of Seahouses, not far from the famous monastery of Lindisfarne. In the harbour you pay to be taken by boat to land on Inner Farne and Staple Islands. They are not far offshore but enough to guarantee safety to tens of thousands of seabirds that nest there.

As you set off from the mainland the islands look tiny and, as you get nearer, you don't get the same impression that you do on the Bass Rock. Not only are these small islands, like Bass, but they are flat and low-lying. Thousands of seabirds nest on these islands and you get the feeling of large numbers already mid-way towards the islands.

The first island that is visited is Staple Island about 6 kilometres from Seahouses. The low cliffs are teeming with guillemots and kittiwakes in particular but there are also razorbills and shags. Atlantic grey seals surface from time to time to inspect you, showing no fear. The seabirds don't care about our presence either. You might think it's because of the safety afforded by the distance between boat and shore but it's actually the same once you're on land.

The boat approaches our landing spot, similar to Bass Rock, and we quickly disembark. We are immediately greeted by nesting shags, fulmars, and a few guillemots. You can go right up to them and they don't flinch. Somehow the birds seem to know that we pose no danger here. It has to be the context. Elsewhere these same birds would not tolerate our proximity but on the island the combination of fixation to the nest and their individual experience of never having been disturbed here seems to do the trick.

Wardens are about to ensure that it stays that way for a long time to come. It may not, not because of lack of protection, but because of our broader activities, such as changing the climate and impoverishing fish stocks.

In fact, the 2016 *State of UK's Birds Report*, published in April 2017 by the Royal Society for the Protection of Birds, highlighted the puffin among the species that were placed on the Red List of species under threat of extinction because of concern at the global scale. Long-tailed ducks and velvet scoters, sea duck we have also met so far, were also added for similar reasons. The report noted that many seabirds were in decline in the UK and kittiwakes and shags were also added to the Red List. It is a sad day when we are told that puffins may face the same fate as the great auk. Clubbing birds on the head is not the only way of driving a species to extinction. Most often it is the surreptitious factors delivered from a distance that are the most catastrophic. There is no point in bemoaning the extinction of the great auk if we are prepared to hide and watch a similar fate for many of today's species, puffins included.

Puffins are the stars of the Farnes. You soon pick them up flying in and out of their nesting sites. Puffins, unlike guillemots and razorbills which nest on the open ledges, enlarge old rabbit burrows and convert them into their nests. If you are there when they have chicks in the nest then you will see them coming back with not one but five or six sand eels firmly held in the beak. Each year the sand eels get scarcer and the puffins spend more and more energy flying greater distances to catch them. This has an effect on breeding success and gradually numbers start to go down. One day there will be no puffins left on the Farnes unless we take serious action to remedy the causes, which are not to be found on the islands themselves.

Back in the 1980s I used to count the numbers of seabirds pass-ing Europa Point, Gibraltar's most southerly tip, as they migrated between the Atlantic and the Mediterranean. The highest count of puffins that I had was 13 000 in five hours on 28 March 1985. This typified the large movements which took place then. In recent years I have gone out looking for puffins around the same time and I have seen very few, even from a boat, from which you would expect to see more than from the coast.

Returning to the Farnes, when the boat takes you to the second island, Inner Farne, you are greeted by hundreds of raucous Arctic terns that seem to constantly protest your intrusion into their territory. It doesn't stop with the incessant screaming—they will dive at you, land on your head (a hat is advisable), and peck you, even drawing blood. Luckily the terns are small (weighing around 110 grams contrasting with the 3-kilo gannets).

On the northernmost of the Shetland Islands—Unst—it is another seabird that you have to beware of. One spring we went up to see the great skuas, predatory seabirds that breed on the island. We asked the warden how close we would be allowed to get without disturbing them, to which the reply was that the birds would let us know. We spent much of the day avoiding the 1.5 kilos of seabird hurtling at us fearlessly. Thinking of the archaeologists once more, we couldn't help but laugh. On Unst, it was we who had to get away from the birds.

There is a stack on Inner Farne where you can approach some of the nesting seabirds so close that you could easily touch them. It is a favourite spot of ours, one of those special places where you can photograph birds without a hide and using a wide angle lens. This sums up the Farnes and reinforces one of the import-ant points that I have been highlighting so far: that birds are not always fast-moving, difficult-to-catch prey. Sometimes you have to get away from them. So long as you are smart enough to know when to be in the right place, you can hit the jackpot.

The Farnes today give us a semblance of a healthy seabird colony even though we know that it has its problems. For now we can continue to enjoy the seabird spectacle while wondering how much more spectacular it would have been for the Neanderthals. Imagine the cliffs of Gibraltar as a kind of amalgam of the Bass Rock and the Farnes. Add to that the large numbers of cliff-nesting raptors and corvids and you have Pleistocene mayhem. Neanderthals capable of climbing the rocks to get to the ibexes would have had no difficulty knowing when and where to raid the seabird nests or taking the birds themselves, leaving no trace of their work in the archaeology.

CHAPTER 10

BIG EYES

The sun sets over the horizon. It is a warm late spring evening, not a cloud in the sky. The sky's colours blend from dark blues through violets and mauves towards a pastel buff with pinkish hue. The noise from the last of the day's cicadas gives way to the incessant 'cric-cric' of the crickets of the night shift. All seems quiet on the dunes as a pair of large yellow eyes cautiously peers from behind a dry shrub.

Eurasian stone curlews (Plate 3) are large, and related to the wading birds, but left the aquatic habit for dry ground millions of years ago. Their remains have also been found in Neanderthal levels in the Gibraltar caves. Their plumage, which has been fine-tuned all this time, is cryptic, a mix of buffs, browns, and blacks put together in patterns of lines and streaks to create an exquisite creature, the essence of stealth. See them before they see you and, reliant on their camouflage, they will allow you to get up close so long as you don't make any abrupt movements. Seeing them first is easier said than done, of course.

Observing birds in Europe, where they have been exposed to human predation for so long, can give us a distorted image. In Australia we found a close relative—the bush stonecurlew— to be bold and allowing a close approach. That may well have been the situation with the Eurasian stone curlews when

Neanderthals were around. Maybe they weren't that complicated to catch after all.

The large eyes of all stone curlews, appearing disproportionate
to the bird's size, are in contrast with the rest of the animal, which
is designed to hide. The eyes give away this bird's habits, which
are crepuscular and nocturnal. They need to see well in the dark.
Neanderthals had big eyes too.

Why did Neanderthals have such large eyes? A recent paper
compared Neanderthal and Modern Human eyes and concluded
that Neanderthals had invested in enhanced vision (assumed to
correlate with eye size) at the expense of the development of the
neocortex, which is so important to cognition[1]. Modern Humans,
on the other hand, had invested in the neocortex instead and this
permitted them to live in larger groups and interact socially with a
greater number of individuals than Neanderthals could. It was yet
another way of demoting the Neanderthals to a level of inferiority
that could explain our superiority over them and their eventual
extinction. A media report on the paper ran the piece with the
headline, 'Neanderthals' large eyes "caused their demise"'[2]. The
paper was rebutted by others on methodological grounds and
concluded that the larger orbits of the Neanderthals compared
to the average modern human population could not permit any
interpretation of cognitive ability based on group size[3].

There are problems with this interpretation. The study deduced
that living in high latitudes, and presumably in lower light, had
triggered this evolution in the size of the Neanderthal eye. How
could this be when the Neanderthals had occupied such a wide
latitude range anyway? Had eye size adapted to the average latitude conditions? At high latitudes day length is very short or non-
existent in winter but long in the summer, so was eye size adapted

to winter conditions? This would assume that Neanderthals did remain in high latitudes in the winter, living in total darkness, something which has not been proved. How could eye size have been selected for under such varied conditions? So, we wondered, could it be something else? Could Neanderthals have behaved like stone curlews, focusing their activities during the twilight hours and perhaps even at night?

I think that there is a lot of mileage in this view. I have previously argued[4] that Modern Humans succeeded in the conditions of the tropical savannahs by focusing their activities in the middle of the day when it was hottest and predators and competitors were asleep. This led to hair loss, sweat glands, and a dependence on water. Neanderthals living in cooler climates than modern humans would not have benefited from middle-of-the-day activities in the same way. Their hunting strategy was one of ambush hunting and what better time to practise it than in the hours when low light made them blend into the background? Geraldine and I have discussed this many times, long before the eye socket paper came out, and we think that the case in favour is persuasive.

Dawn and dusk are the times of greatest activity—a smart Neanderthal would have known that. When we go out to observe birds and mammals we concentrate our effort in the first and last hours of the day. Activity is more pronounced and lasts longer in the mornings than at dusk. There are many more opportunities at these times for a hunter. So it would make sense that humans living outside the hot tropics should spend their energy searching for and hunting prey at those times when prey were most active, with the added bonus that low light would assist in getting close undetected. If we go to the high latitudes in the summer the days practically last twenty-four hours and there is a long twilight period for many months in the spring and autumn. Yet, if you want to spend time observing and photographing bears or wolves, or many other animals for that matter, it is best to sleep during the day and be awake during the night hours (even if these are not dark) when the animals remain most active. So we have an explanation that satisfies all conditions which Neanderthals would have experienced in Eurasia and not just a few.

How do you catch a stone curlew? I haven't really tried but my answer would be, assuming the absence of netting or other technology, by careful stalking during the breeding season. At that time the pair take turns to incubate the eggs and will sit tight. Perhaps the target of hunters would not have been the birds but, instead, the eggs and the occasional zealous nest defender with them. Collecting stone curlew eggs was practiced in Kent, England, in the nineteenth century[5]. Apparently the trade was systematic since each stone curlew pair occupied a traditional territory which was well known to the local fishermen. I'm sure that Neanderthals would have been fully aware of this habit and gone back each year to the old territories for the year's clutch. If indeed Neanderthals operated in the hours of twilight, then they would have been out precisely when the stone curlews were most active and easy to locate.

Are there other birds with characteristics similar to the stone curlew—that is, ground-dwelling and -nesting birds with cryptic plumage and freezing behaviour used to hide instead of flying away? And do we find any of these birds in Neanderthal sites? One bird that immediately qualifies is the red-necked nightjar, which has also been found in the Gibraltar caves. This bird is really hard to find during the day on account of its motionless behaviour and cryptic plumage. It is a species which arrives from tropical Africa in the spring and nests precisely on the sandy ground in pine woods, especially if these are stone pines. The birds are exclusively nocturnal and come out at dusk, to hawk for moths.

Stewart and I have found a way of photographing these birds, and also their close cousin the European nightjar, both of which have similar plumage and habits. We drive along tracks at night and sooner or later we find a nightjar sitting on the ground in front of us, dazzled by the headlights. One of us walks out of the car and photographs the bird at very close quarters, often less than a metre away. We haven't tried but I'm sure that we could catch some of them with our bare hands. We know of a bird ringer who would use this technique to catch nightjars with a pole and a net attached to the end; he could catch quite a few on any single night. Of course, this only works at dusk or at night.

On one occasion I arrived at our lodge on the shores of Lake Victoria in Tanzania and, tired after a long journey, walked along an area of open forest from the reception area to our lodging. The next morning our local guide pointed out nightjar after nightjar on the ground where we had walked the night before. Luckily we didn't tread on any. In this case the species was the square-tailed nightjar, to all intents and purposes displaying similar plumage and behaviour to its European counterparts. Once we 'got our eye in' we were spotting them easily on the ground and getting right up to photograph them. The only difference with the photos we took in Europe at night was that the European birds had their eyes wide open—these were sleeping, oblivious or uncaring of our presence and totally reliant on their plumage to hide them. Neanderthals on the dunes off Gibraltar would have been familiar with these birds at dusk and, living in their world all day and night, would have done better than us on the shores of Lake Victoria. As with the bush stone curlew in Australia, this non-European example shows us how distorted our image can be when relying only on observations of European birds that have been so affected by human predation.

The woodcock is a wading bird that, like the stone curlew, has left a semi-aquatic life, in this case in preference for forests. It has a long, straight bill for probing the soft earth. Though unrelated to either the stone curlew or the nightjars, the woodcock lives on the ground and has a similarly cryptic plumage that allows it to blend in with its background. This is another bird that sits quietly all day on the forest floor and is virtually impossible to find. It becomes active at dusk and forages at night. In the breeding season the male becomes highly visible and audible when it performs a display flight above the forest canopy which is known as roding. Roding woodcocks are seeking to lure females. After mating the male stays a few days with the female, then resumes his roding antics as he sets his eyes on another female. Sit in a forest clearing at dusk and, if there is a woodcock about, you'll soon find him advertising his position to all and sundry.

A relative of the woodcock, and another species found at Gibraltar in association with the Neanderthals, is the snipe. It lives in more open and humid ground than its relative, is also cryptic, and freezes on the ground until the last possible moment. In the spring males perform a drumming flight with the purpose of attracting females and the performance is, once again, crepuscular. It has also traditionally been a bird sought after as food.

There is one more bird which we need to include here. When Geraldine was doing the research for her thesis, she looked at Neanderthal sites in different parts of Europe. One bird kept coming up on the list, in fact in over three-quarters of all Neanderthal sites. It was the quail. These birds have had a long history of being hunted for food by people, particularly in the Mediterranean, so their culinary appeal is not in question. What intrigued us about quail was their behaviour. They are notoriously difficult to see as they hide in tall grass, so could the Neanderthals have somehow caught them for food? Traditional methods have involved the use of nets but we do not know, of course, if Neanderthals used nets as these would have perished long ago, leaving no trace for archaeologists to find.

One evening, Geraldine and I were going on an evening drive in the Biological Reserve at the Doñana National Park. We heard quail calling and suddenly we surprised one on the side of the track. Caught between the open ground and the tall grass it froze and we watched it for a short while before moving on as the sun was now setting and we needed to get back. As we were driven back we commented to the warden who was with us how difficult these birds were to see and how complicated it would have been to catch them. His reply was not what we expected. According to him it was actually very easy.

He explained how, as a young lad, he and his brother caught many quail without need of any special technology but for one crucial item. Many of these wardens are poachers turned game-keepers and they are incredibly knowledgeable about animal behaviour. Talk to them and you discover aspects of behaviour that you won't find in any text book. So what was this important piece of equipment? It was a modified rabbit bone, punctured to create a whistle. During the quail breeding season one brother would stand and blow the whistle to imitate the quail call and the other would stand and wait for other quail to appear in response to the lure. The birds became so fixated on the call that they could catch them with their hands. Only a smart human could have come up with something like that.

Curious to find out more we tried searching the literature. To our surprise there was relatively little to be found and some of the most interesting material went back to the seventeenth century. The great ornithologist Reg Moreau, in a paper published in the journal *British Birds* in 1951[6], cited Markham who in 1621 had written 'when you hear the male byrde call you must answere in the note of the female, and if the female call, you must answer in the note of the male, and you shall be sure that both the one and the other will most busily come about you and never leave till they finde the place whence the sound cometh, to which when they do approach they will stand and gaze and listen till the nette be quite cast over them.' This is astonishingly close to what the Doñana warden had told us.

In the excellent book *Feasting, Fowling and Feathers* Michael Shrubb[5] cites Ray, who in 1678 described how quail were netted in the standing corn by fowlers attracting them to the nets by calling on a quail pipe. He doesn't say what a quail pipe looked like, or what it was made of, but the two seventeenth century references put together certainly support what we had been told.

What these examples tell us is that sweeping statements made by some archaeologists, such as birds are fast-moving prey or hard to catch, are gross overgeneralizations which reveal an absence of natural history understanding, an understanding that intelligent Neanderthals would have had. Each species has to be looked at individually and its biology has to be understood. When looking at mammals attempts are made, although in my opinion still with insufficient detail, to distinguish the types of mammals and how they might have behaved. Generally, when looking at birds in the context of Neanderthal and other ancient human predation, they are all classified as birds without significant distinction. I hope that what I have said so far is sufficient to convince the reader that there is much more to it than that and that we really have to get to know each species individually before we can attempt to interpret data coming out of archaeological sites. With birds the devil really is in the detail.

It seems, then, that a number of birds associated with Neanderthal sites, though themselves unrelated to each other, share features in common. These features include ground-dwelling and -nesting, cryptic plumage, crepuscular and nocturnal habits, and periods when they become conspicuous when engaged in breeding activities. There are other species that might fit into this picture more broadly and which are also found in the Neanderthal caves: female duck of various species, partridges, crakes, some waders, larks, pipits, and sparrows. If Neanderthals had really got their eye into these ground dwellers, then a significant food supply would have been available to them. Given the breeding activities of some of the species and the fact that others (like the red-necked nightjar) would have come in from Africa in the spring, it is tempting to think that the catching of these ground birds and their eggs might well have been a spring activity.

1. Nana and Flint. Forensic reconstructions of the two Gibraltar Neanderthals by Kennis & Kennis.

2. Gorham's and Vanguard Caves seen from the sea today.

3. The crepuscular stone curlew with its strikingly large eyes, Central Spain.

4. Golden Eagle feeding on the carcass of a Red Fox, Central Sweden.

5. Cinereous Vulture in aggressive pose, Central Spain.

6. Lammergeier showing orange plumage caused by bathing in iron-rich pools, Pyrenees.

7. Stewart up close with wild Griffon Vultures, Pyrenees.

8. Excavation inside Gorham's Cave.

CHAPTER 11

DIGGING IN THE CAVE

Having spent much of my life observing and studying birds, I couldn't but help to get increasingly curious with the high species diversity that we were getting out from the Neanderthal caves during our annual excavations. It seemed that every time our specialist came down to have a look at the latest batch of finds several new species turned up. At the time of writing we have recorded 160 species between four Neanderthal caves in Gibraltar[1], the highest avian diversity of any Neanderthal site in the world.

A number of people have worked with the identification of the birds from these caves in the past but in recent years the main researcher has been Antonio Sanchez Marco from Madrid. There are few people able to do what Antonio does and we have been lucky to have him in our team. Every year he drives down to Gibraltar and spends time sorting through the thousands of bones that have been brought from the caves and begins the arduous task of attempting to identify the species to which the bird bones belong.

He does this by comparing the bones with reference collections, although in the case of many of the commoner species he is able to do without need for comparisons, simply because he has seen so many. This would be the case with, for example, rock doves, partridges, or the choughs. The reference collections, such as the one in the Natural History Museum in Tring, England, are invaluable. These are bones taken from present-day specimens that have found their way into the collections. Many of the comparisons are made by identifying key morphological features of particular bones, but size can be an added support. The problem with size is that some species appear to have been larger during the glaciations. In some cases the difference may be attributable to the advantages of large body size in cold climates[2]. In other cases, as with vultures, they may reflect the presence of some very large mammals in the Pleistocene world. Relying on size alone is dangerous in identification.

So how are all the bones retrieved in the first place? We have been working in the Gibraltar caves for 28 years now. Each summer, typically for two months, we have assembled an excavation team. It is usually a mix of youth and experience. Hardened cave excavators are joined by students at various stages in their careers, from undergraduate to post-doctoral, who work under close supervision. The whole excavation is an exercise in planning and logistics as we have to house and feed everyone during this time. Our preferred team size is 25, a magic number derived from years of trial and error. Fewer than this makes the work hard but having more people—and one year we had 60—makes control of the excavation process difficult.

The reason is that an excavation of the magnitude of that at Gibraltar has to be seen as a process which involves three laboratory operations and they all have to be strictly managed. For us the first laboratory is the cave itself. We can't just go in and start digging. We must first get an understanding of the way in which the material inside the cave—the sediment—has gradually accumulated. This is important in order to have a clear understanding of what we are excavating. An example will illustrate why it is so complicated.

Dig an urban site or a site in an open field and the problems are not as complicated as in a cave. Here, material would have typically built up slowly over time. This means that digging a trench would produce a vertical section in which the layers which have accumulated through time follow a clear sequence, oldest at the base, as they were the first to have been deposited, and youngest ones at the top.

The principle is the same in a cave except that the horizontal sequence may not always be as clear. In Gorham's and Vanguard Caves, a lot of sand entered the caves as the dunes moved. This sand progressively accumulated inside the cave, eventually forming deposits that were up to 18 metres thick. As the sand entered the cave it 'climbed' as the wind pushed it against previously deposited sand. Once that sand reached the top it then started slipping downwards due to gravity towards the back of the cave. What we find then is that any particular archaeological level may not be strictly horizontal but may be sloping upwards at the entrance and downwards at the back. We can still follow the archaeological layer but it needs a very experienced excavator to do so. Remember that every time a trowel or brush goes into the layer and removes something, it is irretrievable. Archaeology is inevitably destructive so we must ensure that we retrieve every possible piece of evidence before we lift an item, be it a bone, stone tool, or piece of charcoal.

The first task is to make a complete survey of the cave. This involves the placing of a grid, in our case of 1×1-metre squares, on the floor of the cave. In the old days this was a physical grid, usually wires placed above the excavation itself, with plumb lines dropping from the corners down to the archaeological layer. Each square was given a reference number within the grid. Today we can plot all this with a 'total station', the kind of electronic theodo-lite used by surveyors, without need for the wires. All the same, as an excavator works on his or her square, this is well demarcated on the floor by elastic tape attached to nails on each of the four corners of the square.

The process of selecting which squares to excavate is not ran-dom. Usually the research team discusses the previous year's results and sets out questions which need to be answered. This is done months ahead of the excavation so that when the team arrives on site it has been fully briefed on the objectives for the season. It is vital that all members of the team not only know what they are doing but, importantly, why they are doing it.

The process of excavation is painstakingly slow. The speed at which a square is excavated depends in part on the experience of the person excavating but it also depends on the deposit itself. If the dune came in particularly quickly at that point then it may be that there are few items to be recovered so excavation can be faster than at times when a lot of artefacts are being found. In this lat-ter case the excavator carefully cleans off the sediment around the located artefacts which are not lifted at this stage. The sediment which is removed is not thrown away but kept in bags for sieving. The sieving station is the second laboratory in the operation.

First, let's see what happens to the artefacts which have been located within the square. These may be a few or, as in some layers at Gorham's Cave, hundreds. Recently, we have been digging a series of squares in the middle part of this cave. The area had been occupied by Neanderthals around 48 000 years ago. They came into the cave with an ibex which they butchered and presumably ate around a camp fire. What we found 48 000 years later were the remains of the hearth, in the form of a blackened structure with pale-grey ash on the margins and hundreds of small pieces of charcoal produced as the embers from the fire spat outwards. The remains of the ibex were on the margin of the hearth, some evidently burnt (we could tell even before lifting them and examining them in detail) from having been in the fire. Other fractured bones were scattered here and there, and there were also the remains of shellfish and even the seeds and cases of stone pines, a remarkable piece of preservation. We also found the tools which the Neanderthals had made and used.

Each and every one of these items was positioned within the square and given, with the help of the total station, three co-ordinates X, Y, and Z. X and Y gave the spatial location of each piece within the square. As the square was located within the whole cave grid, we could then place the piece exactly on the whole map of the cave. These spatial co-ordinates are very important when interpreting how Neanderthals may have used the space inside the cave, for example where the bones were relative to the fire, where the tools were and so on. Afterwards we could build a picture of where the Neanderthals themselves had been sitting round the camp fire and where in the cave they had done what.

Taking a broader view, we had previously found another hearth deeper in the cave but the area had fewer bones and little evidence of butchering. A combination of pieces of evidence led us to suggest that the Neanderthals had used the deep part of the cave for sleeping (the bedrooms) and the middle area, where we were excavating, as the kitchen.

The Z co-ordinate gives us the vertical position of each artefact in the entire cave sequence and is, if you like, a measure of when it was placed there. Broadly, the deeper the older. Now some of the items recovered, for example the bits of charcoal, could be used later on to date[3] the occupation of that particular level by the Neanderthals. Bone, bits of stalagmite, mollusc shells—all are potentially datable using different methods[4].

In the case of the layer we were excavating we had not had a chance to do this work. It can take many months after the excavation to obtain this information and it is usually also an expensive part of the work to get a date from a laboratory. So how did we know that our layer was 48 000 years old? Because we had previously dated layers above and below it. Those below fell around the 49 000-year mark and those above around 47 000. So the layer sandwiched in between had to be around 48 000 years old.

Once the entire level in any particular square had been excavated and each item positioned on the XYZ grid, a drawing was made showing where each item was located. The level was then photographed and only then did the process of lifting the artefacts start. This usually took two people, one lifting and the other bagging each item individually with a reference number and its co-ordinates. These items were then taken back to the Gibraltar Museum laboratory (the third laboratory) each night. There, another team would examine, classify, and catalogue each piece.

The second laboratory was the sieving station. This was usually on the beach by the caves. The team here would receive the sediment bags from the individual squares being excavated inside. They would know which square and level this material had come from. The process involved passing the sediment through a series of sieves, each time of finer mesh, by passing water with a hose over the sediment.

I love watching the sieving process. You start with what seems to be a bag of dust and that is clearly what the excavator had seen. Only the larger items were visible to the excavator inside the cave.

As the sieving starts, the dust drains away leaving hundreds of bits of stone (which can be discarded) but also tiny bones and shells and bits of charcoal. This material is laid out to dry, bagged, and also taken to the museum laboratory for later analysis. These items may need examination by specialists, like Antonio in the case of the birds. Others may be diagnostic of particular species of rodent, amphibian, or reptile. These animals are particularly good indicators of climate[5] and can give us a good idea of conditions at the time the Neanderthals had been sitting by the hearth.

Charcoal, too, is very useful. Not only can the pieces be used for dating but dissection of the charcoal and examination under light and electron microscopes can reveal the cellular structure of the plants that had gone into the fire and were now charcoal. We often find the remains of olive wood in these hearths. As olives are typical Mediterranean climate trees, their presence shows that conditions then were similar to today, in spite of the glaciations further north. Snowy owls may have been forced down here by conditions elsewhere but, when they got here, they found themselves among the olives.

Returning to the squares under excavation inside Gorham's Cave, we found that spotted hyenas had scavenged the remains of the Neanderthal feast after they had left. We know this because we found their fossilized droppings (coprolites) all over the site. The idea of excavating 48 000-year old hyena dung may not be everyone's cup of tea but for us it's very exciting. We have found that pollen preserves very well in these coprolites so here we have another way of finding out what plants grew outside the cave at the time of the Neanderthals.

How does pollen get into the droppings of a carnivore such as the hyena? Hyenas hunt and scavenge herbivores. They eat every bit of the animal including its intestines. It is the herbivore which has ingested the pollen and it has reached us, all this time later, via the hyenas who ate the intestines and then deposited the pollen in their faeces.

Returning to the identification of bird bones, these then have found their way to our laboratory either as co-ordinated finds (those carefully mapped out in 3-D by the excavator) or through the sieved material. In both cases we know which square and level each bone came from, so we crucially know where and when. This material then needs to be separated out in the laboratory for Antonio's arrival which may be months later. It is at that point that we start to get to know the species of birds from that particular location in the cave. What is more, as we also know what other animals and plants came from the same area, we can begin to reconstruct the ecosystem, Neanderthals and birds included.

CHAPTER 12

NEANDERTHAL REAL ESTATE

There are many Neanderthal archaeological sites scattered around Europe in particular. This density may be a reflection of population numbers; maybe Europe really was the Neanderthal stronghold. On the other hand, it might only reflect sampling intensity. Traditionally Europe has been well worked by archaeologists and there are vast areas of Asia that have been poorly studied in comparison. I discussed this problem with Stewart and we decided to try a different approach.

Could we separate sites occupied by Neanderthals by the quality of the environment in which they lived? Apart from anything else, it would indicate that they had abilities that helped them discriminate good and bad sites, permanent from seasonal ones. It seemed to us that, in looking at Neanderthal sites, nobody had ever attempted to do this. Instead it seemed that the assumption was that all sites were directly comparable, of equal status in terms of the resources which the Neanderthals could harvest from each site. Archaeologists had, of course, looked at the function of particular sites. Had a site been a hunting station for particular prey or had it been a site which they had chosen because it was close to the raw materials needed for their tools? On the whole we found some of the arguments and deductions unconvincing and they didn't translate in terms of answering the questions which we were interested in. We thought that a fresh approach, using birds, could help us so we decided to have a look.

One of the arguments which has been repeatedly used to separate Modern Humans from Neanderthals is that the former had the capacity for forward planning and also the ability to target particular prey, in other words they could specialize in hunting specific animals in ways that Neanderthals could not (Chapter 2). We were unconvinced by the evidence. Let's take an example. It has been argued that a number of French sites with Modern Human occupation were specialized reindeer hunting sites on account of the overwhelming numbers of reindeer bones found; the proportion of bones of other species being very low[1]. Is this sufficient evidence for specialization? In the absence of information on prey availability we simply cannot say. If a particular site had 95 per cent reindeer bones and reindeer had made up 50 per cent of the available animals in that environment, then the argument might hold. But what if the site was overrun by reindeer and they represented 95 per cent of the animals there? Then there could be no argument for specialized hunting. People would have been hunting animals in the proportion that they were encountered. As there were many more reindeer than other species, more reindeer were hunted than anything else when the presumed early Modern Humans arrived in France. In contrast, the fauna may have been more evenly distributed among various species when the Neanderthals had lived in the same area[2].

We have already seen that as the steppe-tundra spread across Europe, many sites in France came to be dominated by steppe-tundra animals. That suggests to us that what we are observing is humans taking prey according to their availability. What about the Neanderthals? We have also seen that they lived in varied environments, as at Gibraltar, where there was much more of a mix of species. This would mean that Neanderthals, if they were behaving as we thought Modern Humans were behaving, that is, selecting animals according to availability, would be expected to show a less pronounced bias towards particular species. Their world was less dominated by a single species than the world of the steppe-tundra.

The other side of the coin, that Neanderthals specialized in particular prey—the hallmark of being a Modern Human according to some researchers—was something that we could show had actually happened. In the mid-1990s we had excavated a cave high on the Rock of Gibraltar, not far from Gorham's and the other Neanderthal caves at sea level but at a much higher elevation (around 300 metres). Here we found that the vast majority of the bones found belonged to ibex. Now, we would be rightly accused of falling victim to the arguments which we had used to cast doubt on Modern Human hunting specialization if we made a simple assumption: if ibex were the only animals available up on the cliffs of the Rock, which was quite likely, then the high proportion of ibex bones would reflect availability and not specialized hunting. This would be true except that Gorham's and Vanguard Caves were close enough to Ibex Cave (as we had imaginatively called the cave) for us to consider that the Gorham's, Vanguard, and Ibex people were one and the same. We knew that there was a diversity of potential prey on the coastal shelf by Gorham's and Vanguard Caves, and we knew that down there Neanderthals were also hunting red deer, horse, and other herbivores. So it seemed to us that hiking up to the cliffs of the Rock was specialized hunting, requiring forward planning for the targeting of a particular species.

This was probably not the only example of such strategic planning by Neanderthals. During our work in Vanguard Cave in the early 2000s we discovered a level of Neanderthal occupation where the main prey animals were monk seals. This suggested to us that there may have been times when Neanderthals targeted seals. It may have been when they came to shore to have their pups and a number of bones of juvenile seals might support this conclusion. Nobody, until then, had suspected this behaviour from the Neanderthals. I will expand on seal hunting in Chapter 13.

If Neanderthals had capacities that allowed them to strategically plan hunting and other foraging activities, then clearly the quality of the environments in which they lived from one area to another would reflect their ability to pick places with high biological diversity, offering plenty of opportunities for choosing different types of food, hunting and foraging habitat, and shelter, or those with lower diversity but a particular target species where it lived at high density. It was also possible that there were marginal populations just barely surviving or depending on immigrants to keep them going. We cannot judge all sites as equal, but that is precisely what has been done over and over again when looking at ancient sites of human occupation. For us, this distinction was critical in developing new views on how Neanderthals and other humans occupied territories and, ultimately, survived in healthy populations.

In order to achieve our aim we decided to compare the well-studied sites at Gibraltar with another similarly studied site nearby which may have offered different opportunities to humans. We chose Zafarraya[3], a Neanderthal site which had been studied in great detail for many years. Zafarraya, in the Spanish Province of Granada, is a cave located on a limestone ridge not far from Gibraltar, approximately 140 kilometres to the north-east in a straight line. While Gibraltar is at sea level and would never have been far from the coast, Zafarraya is a mountain site, at 1022 metres above sea level and today 25 kilometres from the nearest coast.

Could the birds found in association with Neanderthal archaeological levels indicate differences in the ecology of the two sites? We have already seen the avian richness of the Gibraltar site, with a total of 160 species. These could be subdivided by cave: Gorham's Cave, 151 species; Devil's Tower Rock Shelter, 77 species; Vanguard Cave, 73 species; and Ibex Cave, 23 species. In contrast there was only one cave in the Zafarraya ridge and it had produced 35 bird species. We could discard any bias from sampling effort as Zafarraya was a site that had been studied intensively for many years by a large team. The differences reflected something else.

When we analysed which bird species were present in each site, it became obvious that Zafarraya contained a group of species that were also present at Gibraltar. The difference was that Gibraltar also had many species which were not found in Zafarraya. Over half the species in Zafarraya were cliff dwellers. These were of two kinds: scavengers that were sedentary in behaviour (such as vultures and crows) and migratory aerial insect feeders (such as swifts and swallows) that would have been present only in the spring and summer months. Gibraltar had these birds too but also species typical of wetlands, coastal and marine species, and birds of woodland, scrub, and open ground.

The differences reflected the ecological conditions in the two sites. Gibraltar, at sea level, offered birds a range of habitats which were unavailable in the high mountain site. These habitats were, in turn, available to other animals and the Neanderthals. Part of our analysis compared the individual caves in Gibraltar with each other and also with Zafarraya. It was Ibex Cave, the hunting station at 300 metres up the Rock of Gibraltar where Neanderthals had gone to catch the ibex, which was very different from the other Gibraltar caves and, at the same time, most similar to Zafarraya in terms of the birds found. We were amazed to find that over 80 per cent of the animal bones, many butchered by the Neanderthals, at Zafarraya were those of ibex.

Put together, the results gave us a clear picture. The coastal sites indicated places where Neanderthals had many ecological options available to them. In another study[4] where we looked at the types of stone tools found and also evidence in the form of repeated use of camp fires, we had been able to show that Gorham's Cave had been a site of repeated occupation by Neanderthals. Ibex Cave had, instead, revealed itself as a place where Neanderthals had improvised by selecting a particular kind of flint which may have been available nearby and had improvised tools, presumably for a quick hunt. Vanguard Cave, where they had hunted the seals, although close to Gorham's, also suggested a place visited at times for specific purposes.

We could now add Zafarraya, high up in the mountains, to the list of temporary occupation sites, places where Neanderthals went for a specific purpose. In the case of Zafarraya it is hard to imagine Neanderthals living up there in the winter. The 25-kilometre distance to the coast, which may have been a bit longer when the sea levels were lower, was not insurmountable, so it was perfectly possible that Neanderthals went up to Zafarraya after ibex in the spring and summer in the same way as those from Gorham's Cave went up to Ibex Cave for a similar purpose. Those living in Gibraltar had a much shorter walk. They were living in an ecologically rich land where the various resources were available close by and they moved up and down and along the coast seasonally to tap these as they became available. This was a place of high quality in environmental terms, a place where you had everything you needed close by. In contrast, Zafarraya was a place worth visiting for a particular prey at a particular time of the year. The resources available were limited in comparison to Gibraltar, and probably their own coastal areas down the slopes, but distances were certainly greater between seasonal sites here, probably introducing a greater need for long-distance movement. The Gibraltar Neanderthals had it easy in comparison with those at Zafarraya, and birds had helped us in finding this out. Importantly, the exercise showed us that Neanderthals were smart humans, with a clear knowledge of where resources were located and when to go for them.

It may be possible to carry out a similar exercise comparing other sites across the Neanderthal range where birds were present. This is exciting work in progress which Stewart is carrying out for his PhD but for now we have to stay with the idea that not all Neanderthal occupation sites were of equal status in terms of their ability to support and sustain people. Some places were rich in resources which, if in close proximity, may have permitted a semi-sedentary existence, as at Gibraltar. Other locations would have introduced stresses related to movement across long distances as the Neanderthals had to change camps one or more times during the year. Taking this to an extreme, in situations where the steppe-tundra encroached, as in France, these seasonal movements would have involved traversing longer and longer distances, challenging the traditional Neanderthal way of life, which was to live in relatively small territories[5]. The steppe-tundra, with its lack of cover, did not just make it difficult for Neanderthals to ambush hunt; it also stretched them to the limit by forcing them to roam over increasingly greater distances.

CHAPTER 13

OF SEALS AND LIMPETS

U p to this point we have established that Neanderthals were never far from birds wherever they were living. The species which they came across may have varied from place to place, or within a single locality in response to climate change. Some species with particular features in common, such as cryptic ground-dwelling birds that tend to be most active at dusk or night, appear regularly in association with the Neanderthals but we have not shown that Neanderthals actually exploited them or interacted with them in any way. To do this we needed zooarchaeologists who specialize in understanding the processes that affect bones prior to, during, and after being deposited in the archaeological layers. The discipline is called taphonomy. We turned to them to help us with our work in the Gibraltar caves. First we looked at marine invertebrates, then marine mammals and fish, and finally we turned our attention to birds.

For many years I had been battling with the firmly established view that Modern Humans were defined by a behavioural package which made our ancestors so successful that they expanded from an area of tropical Africa to colonize the world. In the process they replaced all other human populations that had not been blessed with the modern behavioural package. Modernity was something which was exclusive to us. One key feature of that package was the exploitation of coastal resources, from mussels and limpets to seals, and the evidence from South Africa, where Modern Humans had lived around 100 000 years ago, was considered to be the hallmark.

In a paper published in *Nature* in 2007[1], archaeologist Curtis Marean and his team provided evidence of the exploitation of marine invertebrates (e.g. mussels and limpets) by Modern Humans at Pinnacle Point, South Africa. The date of the archaeological layer where the remains of these animals were found was highly significant. The exploitation of these marine invertebrates had taken place around 164 000 years ago. The humans were Modern Humans but, at that stage, they were still in the Middle Stone Age (MSA) and would have still had a long way to go before crossing the 50 000-year Rubicon which Richard Klein and his team (Chapter 2) had argued marked the jump towards behavioural modernity in South Africa. Further strengthening the case that these new results marked an important step in humanity's trajectory, Marean and his colleagues found pieces of red ochre (see also Chapter 17 for further discussion of ochre), some of which had been presumably used for personal decoration, implying symbolic behaviour. They also found bladelets among the stone tools. The production of blades, as opposed to flakes, was one of Paul Mellars' markers of modernity (Chapter 1) so this work claimed to show key features of modern behaviour: a change in economy (moving towards exploitation of marine foods), technology, and evidence of symbolism.

On the one hand Marean's team's results certainly reinforced arguments in favour of pushing the origins of modern behaviour back in time, well beyond the 50 000-year mark. On the other, the people producing these behaviours were Modern Humans.

They were still superior to the Neanderthals, doing things the Neanderthals could not do or had only learnt to do much later. And this change in behaviour that was observed in Pinnacle Point marked the earliest evidence of the coastal adaptation that, it had been argued, generated the geographical spread of modern humans out of Africa by following the coast[2].

It is clear that Marean's team considered that what they were observing at Pinnacle Point was a version of Klein's jump towards modern behaviour, only that it was much earlier than previously thought. It was a way of tweaking the system. At that time the earliest fossil evidence of Modern Humans was put to around 200 000 years ago, so Marean and colleagues commented 'We have identified the earliest appearance of a dietary, technological, and cultural package that included coastal occupation, bladelet technology, pigment use, and dietary expansion to marine shell-fish, and is dated to a time close to the biological emergence of modern humans.' The latter part of the statement, linking the behaviour to the emergence of Modern Humans, is no longer valid, of course, as the latest claims put the emergence of Modern Humans at 300 000 years ago[3]. Here we have another one of those paradoxes, the result of the constant tweaking of narratives, in need of explanation: why did it take Modern Humans over 125 000 years to develop modern behaviours?

But there may be a problem with our thinking here. All this assumes that, just because this is the earliest evidence so far of human exploitation of coastal invertebrates, it represents a change in human behaviour that occurred at that time. One of the features of Pinnacle Point that makes it so special is its topography. Because it is on a steep cliff it luckily survived the sea level rise associated with the global warming that constituted the last interglacial around 125 000 years ago. That sea level rise probably washed out similar evidence from other caves lower down, here and in other places. But, of course, evidence of even earlier use of coastal sites is difficult, perhaps impossible, to find. The further back we go in time the more difficult this task will become. This was John Shea's point about geological attrition (Chapter 2): as we go back in time there will be less and less material preserved for us to find. Pinnacle Point therefore shows us that humans were exploiting coastal resources 164 000 years ago but it does not show us that this is the precise time when humans started to do so. That we may never know.

Of course, we could turn to the comparative method and ask did Neanderthals exploit coastal resources and, if so, how far back were they doing it? If we found comparable behaviours to that of the Pinnacle Point humans then it would raise several important points. If the exploitation of coastal resources was regarded as modern human behaviour would this mean that Neanderthals exhibited modern human behaviour? If that was the case then everyone was modern, so the whole argument about cognitive differences between Modern Humans and Neanderthals would go out of the window. Furthermore, if the exploitation of the coast was the necessary prerequisite for global colonization by Modern Humans, why didn't the Neanderthals achieve similar geographical success?

I sometimes take visitors to see our Neanderthal caves in Gibraltar. These caves were declared a World Heritage Site in 2016, precisely because of the long sequence of Neanderthal occupation, which spanned almost 100 000 years. Visits to the two main caves—Gorham's and Vanguard—are strictly controlled and subject to an annual quota of 120 visitors. This is because, once inside the caves, you have to be very careful where you tread in what are veritable treasure troves of ancient camp fires, artefacts, bones, and a few surprises on the way. I will refer to one in particular in Chapter 21.

We have been excavating in these caves for close to thirty years and we have gradually pieced together detailed evidence of the activities of the Neanderthals when they were in the caves. Entering the large, cathedral-like Gorham's Cave causes an immediate impact on the visitor. They never imagined it to be so big. As we walk up into the cave I pause at a particular location. The eyes are still on the massive void and its formations so what they are about to see is a total surprise. I explain we are in an area of the cave that was occupied by Neanderthals some 55 000 years ago. Then I point at a column and the shell of a limpet. I then point to another one, then a mussel, and soon we see an entire line of sediment full of marine shells. I then point to some flakes that had been crafted into cutting edges by the Neanderthals themselves. Here we have a site where the Neanderthals had stopped to consume marine molluscs which they had collected from the rocky beach nearby. Later, I take them to the beach and show them the living descendants of those ancient mussels and limpets.

This archaeological level is not unique. As we excavate in the caves, ancient floors with marine mollusc shells are commonplace. One particular situation could have been described as 'a day in the life of a Neanderthal group'. The pertinent archaeological level was from Vanguard Cave. Now, a feature of this cave is that sand from the ancient (now submerged) coastal shelf dunes rapidly entered the caves with particular wind conditions. This swift entry of sand covered anything that was exposed in the cave. When we excavated here we uncovered a secret scene, one that had been hidden from all humans for 70 000 years.

We found a camp fire and a scatter of typical Neanderthal tools and mollusc shells. The tiny flakes and stone debris, numbering over two hundred pieces, could be reassembled into a single nodule, which told us that the Neanderthals had brought a previously selected stone with them into the cave and made the tools precisely where we had excavated. While they made the tools they must have started the fire and then put the mussels into the fire. The Neanderthals then left the site and the sand was blown into the cave and sealed the remnants of the Neanderthal shellfish barbecue.

The studies of the zooarchaeologists who have worked with us and have looked at the remains of these ancient barbecues have been vital to us. Their work leaves no doubt that the agent that introduced the shells into the caves was human, in our case Neanderthal. Some indicators of this activity are obvious even to the untrained eye—notches on the rim of limpet shells tell the tale of how they were prised from the rocks on the shore. But microscopic scratch marks caused by stone tools, as animals were cut off from their shells, or indications of burning in the fire are among the evidence that implicates the Neanderthals.

The Neanderthal exploitation of marine molluscs at Gibraltar is comparable with similar behaviour by Modern Humans in South Africa. As we have seen, this behaviour has been implicated in the emergence of behavioural modernity. We have a choice here, which is to accept that the Neanderthals were behaviourally modern, in this aspect at least, or to take marine mollusc exploitation off the list of modern behaviour. If we do the latter then we lose one of the principal causes of modern human geographical expansion along coasts. The interpretation of Pinnacle Point would have to be reviewed.

It might have been argued that the Neanderthals were taking marine molluscs from coastal habitats much later than at Pinnacle Point, almost 100 000 years later in fact. I was collaborating with a team that was looking at Neanderthal occupation of another site. This was a strange location that we would hardly have associated with ancient human occupation. Bajondillo Cave is barely a cave anymore; it is an infill on the side of a small bluff where the sea once reached. It is 90 kilometres north-east of Gorham's and Vanguard Caves. To get to it today you have to go into the centre of one of the Costa del Sol's biggest cities—Torremolinos. Here, among throngs of tourists, there is an entrance to a complex of apartments, behind which, and within the property, is the site.

My friends Miguel Cortes and Marili Simon, now at the University of Seville, had been painstakingly negotiating access and had been excavating here for many years and finally they were going to get their reward[4]. It seems that the Neanderthals had been occupying the site at a time when the coast was closer to it than it is today. Here, as in Gibraltar, they had been collecting and eating marine molluscs, including mussels. Bajondillo showed that the Neanderthals had been eating these animals as far back as 150 000 years ago. The error bars of these dates and those of Pinnacle Point overlapped. Not only were Neanderthals behaving in a similar fashion to Modern Humans, they were doing so around the same time.

Richard Klein and colleagues[5] in South Africa had found that Modern Humans had been consuming Cape fur seals. When they looked at the ages of the seals which had been taken they found that the Lower Stone Age (LSA) humans (which they regarded as behaviourally modern) behaved in a very different manner from the earlier, more primitive MSA humans. What they found was that MSA humans were apparently taking more adult and subadult seals than the LSA people, who took more young animals instead. Their interpretation was that the MSA humans failed to focus their coastal visits on the season of peak young seal availability, behaving, instead, like brown hyenas which scavenged the beach the year round.

We had been working in Vanguard Cave in Gibraltar for a few years when we found an archaeological layer that contained some strange-looking bones. We soon knew what we were looking at. These were the bones of Mediterranean monk seals. These bones were found close to a Neanderthal camp fire, with stone tools, within the cave itself, and mixed with the bones of land mammals—ibex, red deer, wild boar, and brown bear. But further surprises were waiting for us. The seals were not the only marine mammals. We found the bones of two different species of dolphin, common and bottlenose. There were fish remains as well as the shells of marine molluscs. The zooarchaeologists once again got to work with a detailed taphonomic examination of all the bones. There was clear evidence that the Neanderthals had altered the bones, which showed cut marks and indications of burning[6].

Not all the marine mammal bones showed these marks but some did. In any case all the bones were clearly associated with the Neanderthal camp fire. The dating of the archaeological level told us that the activity had taken place during the last interglacial, around 125 000 years ago. These dates made sense to us. This was a time of global warming and the sea would have been very close to the caves themselves so the Neanderthals would have not have had to carry the seal and dolphin remains very far. For us this was irrefutable evidence that Neanderthals were behaving in a similar manner to the people of South Africa, and they were doing so perhaps even earlier than the South Africans.

Klein's team criticized our work[7] because they felt that we had very few bones to show that the practice of taking marine mammals by Neanderthals was a regular and systematic activity. The evidence was being tweaked yet again. For them, the Neanderthals were also behaving like hyenas. We were happy that we had shown that the Neanderthals were exploiting marine mammals a long way back. We could not show how they were getting these animals, especially the dolphins, but nor could the workers in South Africa. We had excavated a very small area of the cave and found young as well as adult seals and two species of dolphin. We had been either very lucky or so much material in such a small area really did reveal something special. The rest of that archaeological level awaits our excavation so time will tell whether Neanderthals behaved like hyenas or not.

The work of the zooarchaeologists had shown us just how capable the Neanderthals had been. We were left with questions that we might never be able to answer. Did they have wooden craft and venture out to sea? Did they have nets to catch dolphins and fish? This might seem far-fetched but, knowing just how biased the evidence is stacked against perishable materials (Chapter 1), we would have to accept that we may never know. Of course that does not mean that they didn't have the technology to venture out to sea and catch marine animals. It just means that we have to keep an open mind to the possibility and not dismiss it. Most important of all, we must not get the limited data at our disposal and make assertions to the contrary.

One thing niggled me. We had so many bird remains in our caves that surely we might be able to find evidence that implicated the Neanderthals. We knew that the zooarchaeologists would have a tougher time finding the tell-tale signs. Imagine the difference between cutting flesh from the leg of a large deer and eating the breast muscles of a small bird. For the bird you just wouldn't need a knife, your hands would do, but what traces would that leave for us to find? Thanks to the marine molluscs and mammals we decided that it was time to take on the birds.

CHAPTER 14

BIRDS OF A FEATHER

A s I write these lines, the number of species of birds whose remains have been recovered from Gibraltar's Neanderthal caves stands at 160. This is a staggering figure which amounts to over 30 per cent of all the bird species of Europe. For a very long time the number of bird remains that we were excavating in Gorham's and Vanguard Caves was a source of awe. At the same time it was puzzling given that Neanderthals were not supposed to have been able to catch birds, as we have seen in previous chapters. If it wasn't the Neanderthals then how were all these birds getting into the caves? Could it be carnivores or maybe a large owl? There were certainly candidates available. In the caves we had found remains of Iberian lynx, wild cat, and red fox. These mammals could have been catching birds and bringing them to the cave. We also had large diurnal birds of prey and owls that could have been doing the job. Among these, peregrine and Eleonora's falcons are bird catchers and the large eagle owl certainly takes a wide range of prey including birds. No one predator could explain the range of birds taken, however, from small warblers weighing under 10 grams to great bustards weighing well over 10 kilos.

I knew that birds were still being taken on the cliffs of Gibraltar near the caves. Peregrine falcons still nest here and they only catch birds in mid-air, from town pigeons to unsuspecting exhausted migrating birds in mid-flight. The eagle owl in Gibraltar seems to have developed a taste for gulls. Often as we descend to the caves we find the carcasses of yellow-legged gulls, wings still attached to the skeleton, which have been taken by the owls the night before. Yet, I found it hard to understand how so many individual birds of so many different species and sizes could have been brought in to a cave by these predators. Certainly the bird remains, which were plenty, found right at the back of Gorham's Cave could hardly have been brought in by birds that would rarely venture so deep.

A thorough taphonomic inspection of the bird bones was required and we needed experienced zooarchaeologists who would be able to recognize the tell-tale signs of Neanderthal activity, if there were any. I was convinced, having got to know the Neanderthals so intimately over thirty years, that the confirmation would be there. I knew that the evidence might not be as obvious as on the bones of large mammalian herbivores, where flint knives would have pierced deep into the flesh, but knives would have been used sometimes at least with the larger birds. Then there should be signs of burning if the birds had been roasted. Little did I realize then what we were going to find.

In 2010 I had been in touch with Ruth Blasco, a zooarchaeologist in the process of completing her PhD at the Universitat Rovira i Virgili in Tarragona. I was interested in her work because in 2009 she had published a paper[1] where she showed evidence of human exploitation of ducks in Bolomor Cave in Valencia. What was particularly interesting was that the duck bones had been found in an archaeological level which was around 150 000 to 200 000 years old. It coincided with a cold period just before the last interglacial, the time of the mollusc exploitation at Pinnacle Point in South

Africa (Chapter 13). The dates and location (in eastern Spain) meant that the humans had to have been Neanderthals.

Working with Ruth in Tarragona was Jordi Rosell, an affable Catalan whom I had known for many years. He was a senior member of the excavation team at the famous Spanish site of Atapuerca. I invited them to Gibraltar to discuss how we could work together to look at the Gibraltar bird collection. They didn't take much convincing. Gorham's Cave was one of the key sites for the study of Neanderthals and they seized the opportunity. I was delighted.

We started working systematically through the collections. We had decades-worth of excavated material so there was no point targeting particular species. It all had to be looked at. The volume did not get any better because each year new material was excavated during the summer months. Late in 2010 it became clear that we had something that merited a closer look. We noticed that bones of birds of prey and corvids[2] were common and they showed clear marks made by the Neanderthals. At that time we were working with other ornithologists. One of these was Juanjo Negro, a researcher at the Doñana National Park in south-west Spain. Doñana had served as a proxy for the coastal habitats outside Gorham's Cave (Chapter 7) and we had been amazed at the close match between Doñana's birds today and those of the ancient coastal shelf at Gibraltar.

Juanjo's speciality was birds of prey and he was excited about the possible link with the Neanderthals. He brought in a colleague of his, Gary Bortolotti of the University of Saskatchewan in Canada. Gary was a cheerful Canadian, full of ideas and keen to get involved in our work. One of his interests was bird coloration and it was he who first noticed that there was a link between the birds of prey and corvids the Neanderthals were taking and the colour black. Almost invariably the Neanderthals were taking birds with black feathers.

As more bones were examined, more evidence came up that convinced us that the Neanderthals had somehow been catching these larger birds, not for food but in order to take their feathers. Wing bones had the most cut marks left by the Neanderthals' tools. There were other markers that also identified human activity on the bones but, in contrast, we found very little to implicate other carnivores or birds of prey. It was clear to us early in 2011 that the Neanderthals were taking birds of prey and corvids for their feathers which, we thought, were then being used for adornment or other similar use. Not only were Neanderthals capable of catching birds for food—Stiner and Klein's inaccessible fast-moving prey—they were using them for symbolic purposes. That put feathers in the same club as pendants and beads, which Mellars had stated was a clear marker of belonging to humanity's premier league.

Because we had so many bones to examine, and because we wanted to present a solid case to such a claim, we delayed publication until we felt we had as much information as possible at our disposal. Then came the shock. In March 2011 a paper was published[3] in *Proceedings of the National Academy of Sciences USA*. It was written by an Italian team headed by Marco Peresani from the University of Ferrara. They had found, in a cave known as Riparo Fumane in northern Italy, unusual human modifications on the bones of bird species that could not be related to feeding or utilitarian uses. The humans implicated were Neanderthals. The birds included some of the birds of prey that we had been looking at: bearded vulture, cinereous vulture, and golden eagle. It also included a corvid that we were also familiar with—the yellow-billed chough. They observed the cut marks and other clues of human intervention only on the wing bones and concluded that it indicated intentional removal of feathers by the Neanderthals. They went on to conclude that the human modifications of the bones indicated an activity linked to the symbolic sphere and behavioural modernity of the Neanderthals.

We were devastated. The knowledge that our results had been replicated in another Neanderthal site, 1700 kilometres from Gibraltar, was outweighed heavily by the knowledge that we had been pipped at the post. In reality it shouldn't have mattered. Here was evidence of the kind that supported our long-standing views about Neanderthal behavioural capacities but, science apart, we are humans and subject to the emotional idiosyncrasies of our species. It seemed that all our hard work had been for nothing. In time, we reflected, regrouped, and returned to the laboratory.

One thing that struck us from Peresani's paper was the small size of the sample. It was really down to three raptor bones of three different species, one corvid and a talon of a golden eagle which had been found previously and not really reported as part of the paper. Thinking of Klein's objection to our seal results, that they were too few and did not reflect systematic hunting, we felt that Peresani might come under fire for similar criticism in a further attempt to tweak the modernity narrative. We had, on the other hand, a much more extensive data set so we decided to move on and finish the paper.

If we needed any further incentive, tragic news of Gary Bortolotti's unexpected death in July 2011 saddened us but also made us determined to finish the paper in his honour. The paper finally came out in the journal *PLoS One* in September 2012[4]. Gary was included as co-author in recognition of his important contribution to the study.

We addressed four questions in our paper. The first asked if the connection between Neanderthals and raptors and corvids was a geographically widespread phenomenon, avoiding criticism that the practice was localized in a particular part of the Neanderthal range. To answer this question we looked at 1699 sites across Eurasia during the Late Pleistocene. These had bird remains, some associated with Neanderthals, others with Modern Humans, and others had no connection with humans (palaeontological sites). The latter became our baseline. We could then ask the second question: if some raptor and corvid species were over represented in human sites compared to palaeontological sites. We also compared Neanderthal sites against palaeontological sites and Modern Human sites.

The results were clear. We could show statistically significant associations between Neanderthals and particular types of raptors and corvids over a huge geographical area. The species associated with Neanderthal sites were those with dark flight and tail feathers and those that scavenged. There was no question that this was not a local phenomenon and we had an idea of the kinds of birds that were mostly connected with the Neanderthals.

We had identified 18 species of raptors and corvids which appeared more in human than palaeontological sites across Eurasia. Of these species, Gorham's Cave in Gibraltar had the highest representation of all sites—16 of them (89 per cent). So we had to look at Gorham's Cave in detail. We decided to combine Gorham's Cave and the other Neanderthal sites in Gibraltar in our taphonomic analysis. To that point we had shown associations between Neanderthals and the birds. Now we wanted to show that there had been direct activity on these birds. Finally, Jordi and Ruth's painstaking work could come to the fore.

They examined 604 bones of 21 species of raptors and corvids associated with Neanderthals in Gibraltar. This was no longer a trivial number exposed to criticism. The bones represented a minimum of 124 individual birds. A number of bones showed cut marks made by Neanderthal tools, others of burning, yet others of overextension and peeling[5] and one even had the tooth imprint of a Neanderthal. In contrast very few bones showed evidence of gnawing by carnivores or rodents or of having been damaged by the digestive action of birds of prey.

When we examined the bones which had been modified by the Neanderthals we found that there was a clear bias towards wing bones. This is what Peresani had found in Fumane. In our significantly larger sample 337 (55.7 per cent) of the 604 bones were wing bones. We concluded that our results were striking because of the number of individual birds in the sample, the number of bird species implicated, and the bias towards wing bones. The processing of bird bones by Neanderthals was not random and accidental but a regular behavioural activity. The activity was related to the extraction of the largest, most durable, and arguably most visually striking elements of a bird's plumage. Our conclusion that this was systematic behaviour was reinforced because we had found that the practice had been taking place in three different caves. In Gorham's Cave we found the evidence in three different archaeological levels spanning a period of over 25 000 years. The Neanderthals were behaving in a very modern way.

Our results, combined with those at Riparo Fumane, showed that the practice was also not localized. The wide geographical association we had shown earlier could be backed up by the taphonomic evidence of direct action by Neanderthals on raptor and corvid bones. This was another way of showing that the behaviour was not random or accidental.

Since we published our paper the list of sites showing Neanderthal activity on raptor and corvid bones has grown. It seems that zooarchaeologists had decided to take a fresh look at sites with Neanderthals and birds and were verifying our results, in the process extending the geographical area of the practice and reinforcing that it was regular and systematic behaviour. In 2012, anthropologist Eugene Morin from Trent University in Canada and zooarchaeologist Veronique Laroulandie from the University of Bordeaux published a paper[6] that showed Neanderthal tool marks on a golden eagle talon at the French site of Combe Grenal and similar evidence in two white-tailed eagle talons at Les Fieux in the Dordogne. In the paper they also reported on another talon, of an unidentified bird of prey, with cutmarks from another French Neanderthal site—Pech de l'Azé IV which had been published in 2009[7]. The dates of these sites revealed that the practice was a long-standing one: 100 000 years ago at Pech de l'Azé IV, 90 000 years ago at Combe Grenal, and somewhere between 60 000 and 40 000 years ago at Les Fieux. In 2016 a French team headed by Veronique Laroulandie[8] added golden eagle, cinereous vulture, and raven to the list from Les Fieux. They also observed raptor talons with Neanderthal tool marks in four different archaeological levels at this site.

In 2015 the Croatian site of Krapina made the headlines with the discovery of what was claimed to be Neanderthal jewellery[9]. Davorka Radovcic of the Croatian Natural History Museum in Zagreb was the lead author of a fascinating paper. In it they showed clear evidence of Neanderthal activity on eight white-tailed eagle talons. The activity—multiple edge-smoothed cut marks, polishing, or abrasion marks—was consistent with the talons having been mounted in a necklace or bracelet. What was really stunning about the discovery was the date when the talons had been worked on—130 000 years ago. This added to the evidence of Neanderthal modern behaviour prior to the last interglacial 125 000 years ago. In fact these behaviour patterns had not even been found in Modern Humans in South Africa. What is more, the Neanderthals had been practising this art tens of thousands of years before any Modern Human had reached Europe so they couldn't have learnt the behaviour from newly arrived Modern Humans.

In March 2017, a team that included Francesco d'Errico of the University of Bordeaux, who we will meet again later, published a raven bone fragment from the site of Zaskalnaya VI in the Crimea dated to between 38 000 and 43 000 years ago[10]. Here, Neanderthals had made seven notches on the bone and d'Errico's team were able to show, through experimentation on the bones of domestic turkeys, that the makers had aimed at producing parallel, equidistant notches. It showed that the Neanderthals had aimed to produce a visually consistent pattern. It was the first case of a bone from a Neanderthal site whose modifications could not be explained as a result of butchery activities. This was clearly symbolic behaviour.

We have come a long way in a very short time since the first reports of Neanderthal intervention on the bones of raptors and corvids in 2011. We now know that the practice lasted for around 100 000 years. It was geographically widespread, from Gibraltar in the extreme west to, at least, Crimea in the east. It revealed activities that showed the symbolic capacities of the Neanderthals. One of Paul Mellars' hallmarks of modern human behaviour, arguably the most important one, could no longer be denied of the Neanderthals. If that wasn't enough, we could now feel confident that modern human behaviour in the Neanderthals predated the 50 000-year old Modern Human revolution by over 80 000 years.

CHAPTER 15

THE GOLDEN EAGLE

I still remember the first encounter with the beast. Geraldine and I had prepared for a moment that, as it turned out, we were unprepared for. We had arranged to spend the day up a mountain inside a photographic hide. We were in south-eastern Spain in the Province of Murcia. Our guide, whom we had never met before, picked us up an hour before sunrise and drove us up dark and windy mountain roads. Eventually we came to halt in some kind of widening of the road that posed as a layby. We got our heavy kit out and followed. Walking up a rocky mountain path is not particularly easy when you are unfamiliar with the terrain, you have a hefty pack on your back, and have only a head torch to show you the obstacles along the way. In the end, after a long trek we got to the box-shaped wooden hide that would be our home for the day. We went in and quickly sorted ourselves out as our guide closed the door, locked us in, and left.

The mists of first light soon revealed themselves and we knew that sunrise was not far away. Now we could see a little bit better than when we arrived so we made sure our tripods, cameras, and lenses were all ready for the moment we had been anticipating for so long. We knew it might be a while yet. These beings of the wilderness needed the sun to warm up their world first. Eventually the sun came up and slowly evaporated the morning mists to reveal, for the first time, where we were. It was a ridge. In front of us were some large rocks that formed the spine of the mountain. On one of them was the carcass of a Barbary sheep that had been left by our guide as bait.

We were 1100 metres above sea level here. The Mediterranean Sea, and its beaches thronging with tourists from the north, was some 40 kilometres away. It is wonderful how altitude adds to the solitude afforded by distance. Here we were delightfully alone. As the last wisps of mist finally relinquished their grip we could see distant peaks separated from us by a 500-metre abyss. A tiny Dartford warbler, long tail raised vertically, perched on a juniper close to us. Later a ring ouzel—a migrant from the north that spends the winters in these mountain peaks—was equally oblivious of our presence as it searched for ripe hawthorn berries. Time passed.

Sitting in a hide waiting for something to appear needs a special kind of patience. I am a restless person, rarely able to stay sitting down for very long. I am also easily distracted. Yet, when I get into a hide it all changes. I can spend the whole day in the cramped space and my focus is exclusively on the task at hand. I guess it's what the hunters of the past excelled at doing. Your attention has to be absolute and uncompromising. Things can happen in a split second, without warning, and if you are not ready you go hungry or, in my case, without the picture I had come for.

It was getting close to two in the afternoon. We had been waiting for over six hours and thoughts of failure were creeping into our minds. This is the worst moment, when you begin to lose your concentration. It is difficult for me to describe what happened next—some experiences are constrained by words. The best I can do is to say that something moved in the distance, horizontal with us, against the olive-grey backdrop of the mountains opposite.

Then it was gone. In that split second I knew what it was. Birders call it 'jizz', that indescribable gestalt that cannot be explained in a field guide and is fashioned after years of observation. I shook Geraldine's arm and signalled to her. Silence was essential to the success of our mission.

I knew that it was coming but, even then, I wasn't ready. Out of nowhere it came. One moment the rocks in front of us had nothing but the carcass and the next a huge mass of feathers, muscle, talons, and beak—a quintessential leviathan—stood there, barely 14 metres away. It was a female Golden Eagle, one of the largest and most powerful of birds of prey. In an instant I understood. I understood so much. If I had read an infinity of books they could never have told me what this moment was transmitting. In that second I saw and felt the power of the eagle, I became one of countless generations of humans who over millennia had experienced the same feeling, and I was at one with them all. It was a spiritual experience that will remain with me for the rest of my life. And I felt the Neanderthals closer than they had ever been. Time stopped that instant in the mountains of Murcia and I cried.

So what was it that I had seen that convinced me the eagle was coming? It was a combination of shape and motion, the moment when the eagle folds its wings and drops. Where did it go during those seconds of anticipation? It dropped to gather speed with the help of gravity. With a turn of the wings and tail, without beating its wings, it would have then shot vertically upwards, better than the best of fighter jets, to land on its perch. To us it was an apparition.

Time really did stop (Figure 9). For a second or two, maybe more, we were mesmerized and forgot about our cameras. Such was the spell that the eagle had on us. After those magically

Figure 9 Eye contact with the female golden eagle.

intimate instants we became twenty-first-century humans once more and took myriad pictures of the bird feeding on the carcass of the sheep. Somehow the photographs felt empty, as is so often the case, in comparison with the experience itself. A short while later the smaller male arrived and stood close to his partner hoping to be allowed a morsel or two. In raptors, females are always larger and more powerful than males. Although many theories have been put forward to explain this sexual dimorphism, nobody really knows why it is like this.

The birds left as stealthily as they had arrived, by confidently plunging back into the chasm. We never saw them again. Our stay in the hide, until after sunset so as not to reveal our presence to the eagles that were undoubtedly watching even though we couldn't see them, was a full twelve hours. We got twenty minutes with the eagles and that is the way of things in the wild. You spend hours of emptiness to be rewarded, and then not always, by a few enchanted glimpses of another world. Was this the world that the Australian Aboriginal people call the Dream Time? If it was, then we had been transported to it by the eagles that treasured day.

Evidence of direct intervention on the bones and talons of golden eagles by Neanderthals has now been found in Gibraltar, Italy, and France. This powerful raptor must have had a special place in Neanderthal culture. Seeing how much impact the power of this bird can have on the human mind when seen at close quarters, this is hardly surprising. It is also understandable that it had, and continues to have, such a special place in Native American culture.

Thomas Mails in his magnificent book *The Mystic Warriors of the Plains* gives us a detailed account of the place of the golden eagle in Native American culture in the eighteenth and nineteenth centuries, full of insights into the relationship between human and eagle. They show how much the powerful bird was a part of the daily lives of people. We can only wonder how Neanderthals saw golden eagles but we can be fairly sure that it had a special place in their culture too.

Mails tells us that 'in the mind of the Plains warrior the male golden eagle flew above all the creatures of the world and saw everything. Nothing matched his courage and swiftness, and his talons had the strength of a giant's hand. The eagle was very holy. He was the solar or sun bird, and his feathers were regarded as the rays of the sun. When one or more were worn on an Indian's head or carried as a fan in his hand they established a connection between man and the Great Mystery. Indeed, they brought God's presence as the sun sends shafts of light to earth, and in the union of the eagle and the man, the man became, he thought, as holy as the bird.' I find the reference to the talons particularly interest-ing. In the air the eagle's feathers stand out, but what has always impressed me about the bird when close to it on the ground are its powerful legs and talons (Plate 4).

Those talons and the grip that the eagle can exert are what give the bird its advantage. With it a golden eagle can catch a wide range of prey. Across much of Eurasia medium-sized animals are preferred. They include rabbits, hares, and grouse[1] but the range of prey includes young and adult roe deer, red deer, reindeer, chamois, and fox. Foxes are hunted regularly by Mongol Kazakhs[2] using trained golden eagles. Less well-known is the practice of fly-ing specially selected eagles onto wolves[3] and even wild boar. If the eagle gets a grip with one of its talons, it will hang on to the wolf until it submits out of exhaustion.

Returning to Mails' account of the Plains Warriors, he continues 'Always a wise and cautious bird, the eagle could seldom be caught with a snare or shot with a bow and arrow. In fact, due to its reli-gious significance, the Indian warrior who wanted to use an eagle as a holy medicine or to make a bonnet was not permitted to kill it with a weapon anyway. So the capture of eagles became a sacred act in itself. Dangerous as it was, warriors caught eagles with their bare hands in eagle pits.'

The practice was apparently widespread throughout the Plains. The ethnographer Gilbert Livingstone Wilson dedicated a 245-page treatise to the eagle-hunting practice of the Hidatsa in an account written in 1928[4]. Such was the complexity of the ritual. The essence of the trapping was that a pit was dug into the ground. The location was chosen close to where an eagle lived, usually high on a hill. A warrior would hide inside the pit which would be covered with branches and sticks. Bait, such as part of a deer, was firmly tied to the cover of the pit. Then the lone warrior would be left in the pit to wait for the eagle to land on the bait. This is how Mails described how the Sioux undertook the task:

'By sundown, if he was fortunate, he (the warrior) would catch several birds, although on some days he might not catch any. As they lighted, the eagles were seized by the legs, drawn into the pit, and killed by twisting their necks. Then they were placed on a bed of sacred sage at the foot of the pit. At the end of a successful day the happy warrior left the trap and returned with his eagles to the purifying lodge. Placing the birds in a row, he took a sweat bath in thanksgiving.' The Blackfoot version of the ritual is interesting because of the use of the stuffed skin of a wolf or coyote to make it appear as if the bait was being eaten. According to Mails, 'when an eagle saw the meat from afar he would "boldly" descend to wrest it away from the wolf.' A similar procedure to the Sioux method of capture would follow.

What drew me to this last excerpt was the link with the wolf once again. I recall a personal experience with a Spanish imperial eagle, a close relative of the golden eagle and similar in size and power. In fact they are so similar that I have observed a thirty-year old large female imperial eagle driving away a pair of golden eagles from a rabbit. Usually the golden eagles are the more powerful of the two but this example shows that the roles can be reversed.

Stewart and I were sitting in a hide in a remote location in the Sierra Morena mountains which separate the southern Spanish Region of Andalucia from the rest of Spain. Bait had been placed to entice a pair of imperial eagles down so that we could photograph them. The bait consisted of several chicken carcasses which the eagles adore. These were firmly tied to branches to prevent the eagle from simply carrying the food away. The female eagle arrived soon enough and sat on the crown of a pine tree some 500 metres away. There it sat, and sat and sat. It could see the food but it wasn't coming down.

After a few hours we were beginning to think that this would not be our day. The eagle knew the food was there and seemed uninterested. Then, out of the corner of an eye Stewart saw a fox slowly, but very obviously nervously, making its way towards one of the chicken carcasses. It managed to prise it off and started walking away with it. At that point the passive eagle stirred, looked at the fox with a typically bobbing head motion that I presume allows it to zoom in on the target, and took off in a stoop towards the fox. It took a swipe at the fox, which froze, and then landed right beside it. It confronted the fox, wings outstretched and beak open as it 'barked'[5] at the fox. The confrontation lasted several minutes. We were in awe, seeing the power and audacity of the eagle. Its aim was not to kill the fox but to retrieve the chicken. In the end it succeeded. The fox took the opportunity of the eagle's interest in the meat which it had dropped and dashed away into the forest. The eagle proceeded to take the bait and we were left breathless at what we had seen (Figure 10).

Recalling the foxes that we had seen at this site on previous occasions we realized that most of them had visible injuries. One had had an eye gouged out, another had half an ear missing, and several others had scars in areas of the face. Clearly, the encounter that we had seen had not been a one-off.

Experiences like these were gradually forming a picture in our minds. All published accounts suggested that the Neanderthal preference was for ambush hunting large mammals from cover[6]. Once in close, they would use their thrusting spears to despatch the prey. If this was indeed so, then could they have approached

Figure 10 Stand-off between imperial eagle and fox.

eagles in a similar way, waiting for them to come down and then seizing them, perhaps in a similar way to the Hidatsa, the Sioux, or the Blackfoot? That might seem far-fetched but let's ask ourselves this question. If we hadn't had the observations of the ethnographers, who recorded what they saw, or the verbal narratives of the people themselves, would we have ever known that the Native Americans caught eagles, let alone how they did it? I suggest that the answer, if it depended on the archaeologists, would be no. There would be no material evidence left of the ephemeral practice that relied almost completely on perishable materials. No trace would be left and the archaeologists would conclude, as they have done for the Neanderthals, that it would have been impossible for a Native American to have caught a fast-flying prey, especially one as powerful and dangerous as the golden eagle.

CHAPTER 16

AMBUSHING THE
SCAVENGERS

It's clear from what we have seen so far that the traditional tech-niques and methods applied by archaeologists are insufficient when trying to answer questions about some aspects of human behaviour, especially when looking at a distant past. We have already seen the benefits of a natural history approach. This approach, in combination with taphonomic work, can really advance our understanding of human behaviour in the Pleistocene.

Stewart has been thinking a lot about the problems related to Neanderthal exploitation of birds. It is his PhD subject after all. It was while sitting in a hide watching griffon vultures feasting on a carcass, and then seeing a golden eagle arriving and the vultures fleeing in panic, that he came up with the idea. Could it be that the Neanderthals had observed such scenes while approaching a carcass? Had they translated the image into a way of catching the raptors?

With half an eye on proceedings outside the hide, our impro-vised brainstorming session went something like this. Humans would long have been aware of the presence of vultures in the sky. They would have known, just as we did, that a characteristic change of attitude in the sky, followed by a partial folding of the wings, lowering of the legs, and slight raising of the tail meant a rapid descent towards a fixed point on the ground—undoubtedly a carcass. Vultures watch each other in the sky and, when one bird plummets, the others rush in. It can be extremely fast. Humans would have then had the challenge of rushing to the site before the vultures picked the carcass clean. Other animals would also have learnt to observe the vultures, hyenas in particular. So an intricate network of hunting and scavenging would have developed between the various players. Sometimes humans would have made a kill and would have been aware that the vultures above would make a beeline towards their kill in the hope of scraps. The humans would have known that the vultures' behaviour would attract other, unwanted, characters including the hyenas.

This is probably why we find, for example, so many butchered bones of large mammals in our caves in Gibraltar, as happens in many other sites. The humans, Neanderthals in this case, would have eaten what they could quickly on site and then brought back tasty morsels to the cave where they could consume them in relative safety with the added protection of fire. It was a kind of uneasy symbiosis. Humans were drawn to sources of food by vultures; vultures, and hyenas if they could be kept at bay, would benefit from human kills by taking the scraps.

In 2015 we excavated a 50 000-year old Neanderthal fire within Gorham's Cave. They had butchered and roasted the remains of an ibex that they may have caught close by on the cliffs. Then it seems that they left. The hyenas came in and scavenged the leftovers. We know this because they left their droppings, which had fossilized into coprolites[1], on the surface of the archaeological level, just above (and hence just after) the Neanderthal occupation horizon. So hyenas did benefit from Neanderthal activity too.

Coming back to kills out in the open, humans would have arrived at times when vultures were already there. Instead of rushing in they may have waited to see if any dangerous carnivores were about. In one of those millennially ephemeral instances a golden eagle swooped in to drive the vultures away, just as we had just seen ourselves. At such close quarters they would have been in awe of the powerful bird with its massive talons.

The taphonomic work had clearly shown that birds of prey were being taken for their feathers by the Neanderthals so we wanted to figure out how they might have done it and also when. Was the practice something that they did all year or was it something that happened at a specific time of the year? If it was the latter, then it would further show that Neanderthal behaviour fitted the modern criteria of the archaeologists. Recall that Klein's distinction between MSA and LSA seal-hunters in South Africa had to do with the LSA humans targeting young seals at a specific time of the year, with the poor MSA people just stumbling along, scavenging seals just like brown hyenas did.

The outcome of our conversation in the vulture hide that morning was a paper that Stewart and I published in 2016[2]. We examined 192 Neanderthal sites and 395 Modern Human sites from Eurasia which had raptor and corvid bones in human contexts. Although we were looking at association of species with Neanderthals and Modern Humans we now had good taphonomic evidence of direct intervention by Neanderthals on fourteen species. Nine (56.25 per cent) of these we found were amongst the sixteen most represented at the sites that we examined. Considering the difficulty in finding bird remains and then finding evidence of human activity on these bones, this is a really high proportion of species. If we only looked at raptors, then we found that we had evidence of Neanderthal intervention on five (71.43 per cent) of the seven most highly represented species at human sites. These were golden eagle, white-tailed eagle, bearded vulture, cinereous vulture, and griffon vulture. Was it a coincidence that these were the largest birds of prey that the Neanderthals would have regularly come across in their geographical range? In terms of ranking these raptors by how frequently they appeared in Neanderthal sites, golden eagle topped the bill, followed by cinereous vulture and then the other three species in equal proportion.

Stewart and I arrived by train in the Swedish city of Vasteras where our guide Daniel was waiting for us. We had earlier flown into Stockholm airport from London carrying a heavy load of camera gear. The plan was to drive north to the Black River Valley in central Sweden. It was February and there was snow everywhere. Driving through the vast coniferous forests in the snow, with the occasional moose or roe deer to keep us entertained, was a spectacle in itself. We spent the night in a charming country house and went early to bed.

The next morning we were up very early. It was dark, and very cold. The starlit sky was so clear in this atmosphere and away from the cities. After a hearty breakfast we were being driven to our site across dark country roads and tracks until we reached a spot where Daniel stopped. From here on we had to walk. There was half a metre of snow on the ground and even with snow shoes, which we weren't used to using where we came from, the 500-metre walk in the dark seemed endless. My head torch was firmly shining on Daniel's footprints. In this way I ensured I kept to the invisible path which he was shaping as we went along. We were in a peat bog and the cover of snow hid the uneven surface below.

We finally got to our hide. It was a hide like we had never seen, beautifully crafted in wood, with comfortable chairs and fleeces, a paraffin heater, and even warm slippers to wear once we removed our heavy boots. On the walls were shelves with ornithological magazines and notebooks for us to record our observations. In a small room to one side was a toilet with a bag of peat to use after each visit. Daniel left and, as we were by now used to, we waited in the dark. The paraffin heater took a while to warm up so we kept our layers of clothing on. By the time Daniel returned for us in the evening it was so hot that we were down to T-shirts.

Dawn broke as a thin strip of orange below a line of distant clouds. As it got lighter we had our first glimpse of the snow-covered bog. It was an empty, treeless space. In the distance, a mile or more away, was a line of trees marking the edge of the forest. To either side of us we could see clusters of birch trees showing us that we were on the very edge of the swamp. A short distance in front of us was the carcass of a red fox which Daniel had carefully placed as bait. Daniel regularly collected road kills which he did not let go to waste.

An hour after first light we saw the first one. A massive, broad-winged eagle flew past without any apparent intention of stopping. We readily identified it as a white-tailed eagle, a sea eagle and a close relative of the American bald eagle. It was one of the key species that Neanderthals took. Others flew past until one decided to land on a bare tree which stood alone in the peat bog. It seemed to be the signal for others to follow and soon we had three or four of them close to the fox, sitting on the snow and eyeing each other to see who would make the first move. Their behaviour reminded me of vultures at a carcass. They were huge, bigger and bulkier than golden eagles, with massive beaks. They appeared restless.

The visual negotiation that was taking place among the white-tailed eagles came to an abrupt end when a young golden eagle arrived and took a jab at the first sea eagle in its path. It perched on the lone tree from where it dominated the fox carcass. The rest was a matter of time as the golden eagle took possession of the prize. At the height of the activity we had two golden eagles and eight white-tailed eagles down at the same time, an indescribable spectacle. Only when the first golden eagle retired satiated and the other one had gone did the white-tailed eagles get a chance at the remains (Figure 11). At that point it became every eagle for itself. We thought of how a Neanderthal watching this gathering, with all the toing and froing and the antics of the mighty golden eagle, with its agility, powerful talons, and character, dominating all and sundry, would have interpreted it all.

There are no vultures in Sweden and the eagles seemed to have taken on the role of scavengers. What we were seeing fitted into a

Figure 11 The white-tailed eagle.

wider picture that included vultures and other birds of prey, and of course corvids. In our paper we were eventually able to show statistically that the birds most associated with the Neanderthals and with clear evidence of Neanderthal activity were scavengers. Not all of them were year-round scavengers. Only the vultures were restricted to this method of feeding all year. Golden eagles only scavenge in the winter months and switch to hunting as soon as they start breeding in spring. White-tailed eagles catch fish, in rivers, lakes, and the sea, during the breeding season and also scavenge, only in the winter. So if we were correct and Neanderthals were ambushing the big birds as they came down to carrion, then they could only have been doing so in the winter months. That felt like a revelation.

It was quickly followed by another. We had wondered why two scavenging species that would have been abundant at the time of the Neanderthals—the Egyptian vulture and black kite—seemed to be almost entirely missing from Neanderthal sites. Then it hit us. Of course they weren't. These two birds are highly migratory. They cross the Sahara Desert to spend the winter months in the tropical African savannahs. If the Neanderthals were practising eagle and vulture ambush hunting in the winter they would never have come across these birds which would have been thousands of kilometres to the south.

The confirmation that scavenging was involved was further corroborated by another eagle—the Bonelli's eagle. This eagle, smaller than the golden but nevertheless extremely powerful, specializes on catching medium-sized birds, especially partridges and also pigeons. Today they get themselves into trouble by going for chickens in farms. They rarely scavenge. So, even though they were resident and would have been available in winter, the chances of getting them down onto a carcass would have been very low.

At the end of our study, which started with that simple observation in the natural world, we felt that we had been shown something special, a window into the past. The taphonomy had undoubtedly helped us along the way but it was by getting out into the field and observing the birds and how they behaved that we got the inspiration and also the understanding. There was another important conclusion to be drawn. Not all birds are the same or behave in the same way. It was time to drop the idea that all birds could be classified into a single type (such as fast-moving). The Neanderthals were great naturalists as their lives depended on it. Aware of the beautiful complexity of Nature they would have laughed had anyone simplistically suggested to them that all birds could be lumped into a single entity according to their powers of locomotion. That false notion could only have originated in a world divorced from Nature.

CHAPTER 17

THE BIG SIX

I was on the island of Fuerteventura, at 28°N, in the Canary
Archipelago one autumn. Down there it was like summer.
Fuerteventura, and Lanzarote to its north, are the easternmost of
the Canary Islands. Barely 100 kilometres off the north-west coast
of the Sahara Desert, Fuerteventura's landscape is dominated by
extinct volcanoes and desert. The typical birds here are those of
the world of aridity: the presence of the houbara bustard, cream-
coloured courser, and trumpeter finch reveal that, climatically and
ecologically, this is an Atlantic island extension of the great desert.

In spite of all these exotic bird species, it was a much commoner
one that caught my attention one day. I was up on the slopes of
one of the volcanoes when a familiar croaking cry filled the air.
Soon I found them: a pair of ravens playing with the wind that was
buffeting the rocky slopes. Fuerteventura means strong wind, a
characteristic of these islands, and the ravens seemed very much
at home here. Opportunistic scavengers and predators, the desert
conditions did not faze them at all. When you don't specialize on
a particular range of foods or places in which to live, you can be at
home in many different worlds.

On another occasion, Geraldine and I were on a zodiac inflatable boat in Disko Bay, north-west Greenland, at 69°N and
5000 kilometres north-west of Fuerteventura, right on the other

side of the Atlantic. We had been floating on sea ice while winding in and out among towering icebergs. The birds that were about were those we might expect up here: kittiwakes, Iceland and glaucous gulls. The overall tone of the birds matched the white of the rest of the landscape. A tiny black speck right at the very peak of the tallest iceberg, completely out of sync with the rest, caught our eye. We looked at it through binoculars to find that we were looking at a raven.

In Chapter 6 we had a brief glimpse at the raven, the largest of the corvids, or crow family. We saw how it lived on the cliffs of Gibraltar, as it still does today, and acted as an early warning system to vultures of the arrival of the feared golden eagle. Like the golden eagle, the raven is the largest member of its family to be found across much of Eurasia and North America. These two species are the most geographically widespread of their respective families and frequently occur together in the same habitats and contexts, particularly in the winter where there is a carcass or in spring on cliffs where both nest.

We have seen that the golden eagle was a regular feature of Neanderthal sites but the raven was even more. The Neanderthals could have accessed them at carcasses when they went after the big raptors but these highly intelligent and wary birds may have been much more difficult to catch this way. On the other hand, their boldness would have brought them close to the Neanderthal camp sites in search of scraps. There would have been a long history of ravens following Neanderthals, and probably earlier humans, across the landscape. These birds would have learnt, from a very early stage, that this practice would have brought its rewards by way of ample scraps and leftovers[1].

In Chapter 14 we saw that there is direct evidence of Neanderthal intervention on raven bones from more than one site and it includes a recent discovery of what is apparently a symmetrical pattern of grooves on a fragment of bone from a raven. There can be no question, therefore, that there was a deep interrelationship between ravens and Neanderthals. We cannot comprehend what that connection might have entailed but the long-standing relationship between us and these birds can give us clues.

For the Native Americans of the plains[2], the raven was a bird of great wisdom, telling of forthcoming events, leading them to prey and warning of impending danger. For those tribes in the Pacific Northwest[3] the raven was central to their symbolic vocabulary and part of their collective world vision. Raven representations for these people were often of monumental proportions, such as on the prow of magnificent canoes or at the crest of totem poles.

Probably more than any other bird the raven has held a notable place in the minds of people in the northern hemisphere and how they saw the world[1]. Ratcliffe provides a comprehensive account that shows the degree to which ravens entered our world of myth and legend. He provides a wonderful quotation by R. Bosworth Smith[4] which summarizes beautifully the raven's place in history:

"A bird whose literary history begins with Cain, with Noah, and with Elijah, and who gave his name to the Midianite chieftain Oreb; whose every action and cry was observed and noted down, alike by descendants of Romulus and the ancestors of Rolf the Ganger; who occurs in every second play of Shakespeare; who forms the subject of the most eerie poem of Edgar Allen Poe, and enlivens the pages of the *Roderick Random* of Smollett, of the *Rookwood* of Ainsworth, of the *Barnaby Rudge* of Dickens, is a bird whose historical and literary pre-eminence is unapproached."

The golden eagle and the raven had pre-eminence in Neanderthal culture judging from the number of locations where the three coincided and the direct evidence now showing that Neanderthals took them. I have described the nature of the relationship with the two species, which would seem to have its similarities and also differences: the golden eagle is the ubiquitous symbol of power while the raven signifies intelligence and guile; the two species were associated with scavenging, which may explain how they were caught but the raven's sharpness may have made it more difficult to capture than the eagle; on the other hand the raven's confidence would have brought it closer to Neanderthals in a wider range of scavenging situations, such as picking scraps from camp sites, which may have been its downfall.

In Chapter 16 I listed four other raptors that we now know had been directly handled by Neanderthals and which were also commonly associated with them, although less so than the golden eagle and the raven. The difference may have had to do with the importance attached to each species or it may reflect the wider geographical ranges of golden eagle and raven compared with the other species. If it is the latter, then the dominant presence of golden eagle and raven at Neanderthal sites may just be a reflection of greater chance of contact between them.

What is clear is that these other four raptors—cinereous, bearded, and griffon vultures, and the white-tailed eagle—completed a suite of 'special' species for the Neanderthals. The white-tailed eagle seems to have been taken for its magnificent talons as well as its feathers (Chapter 14). We saw in Chapter 16 that, despite its large size and power, it seemed to defer to the golden eagle when the two were together. Its habits, and its large size and massive beak (ideal for tearing hide and flesh) remind us of a vulture rather than an eagle. It is, in fact, Europe's largest bird of prey after the vultures. In the north of Eurasia, where vultures are absent today, the white-tailed eagle performs the role of vulture in the winter. The situation may have been different in Neanderthal times as there is clear evidence that vultures wandered further north, even into Germany, than today. Presumably the large herds of reindeer and woolly mammoth at that time drew these birds in from the south.

The white-tailed eagle seems to have been, in Anglo-Saxon and Norse literature, the companion of the raven as a carrion-feeder at battlefields[5]. The white-tailed eagle is much more sociable than the golden eagle and will form large gatherings where there is a concentrated food source so their attendance at battlefields is no surprise. On Hokkaido Island, Japan, hundreds will gather to take offal thrown overboard from fishing boats[6] in winter. On the coast of western Scotland, prior to 1871, before they were ruthlessly persecuted to extinction, gatherings of up to forty birds were recorded attracted to carrion[7]. Its North American relative, the famous bald eagle, still gathers in great numbers today in the salmon-spawning grounds of Alaska[6].

The Anglo-Saxon name for this eagle—Erne—seems to have been retained in some Victorian ornithological works. The Norse equivalent is Ørn and it appears in a number of poems. The expressions 'to give the eagle food' and 'feed the eagles' were kennings[8] for 'kill enemies'[5]. They appear in rune-stones commemorating battles, for example, and the lines in Olaf of Sweden's Praise tell that 'Olaf feeds the eagles; the lord of the Swedes is foremost. The erne drinks his supper; the she-wolf laps the blood; the wolf stains his jaws; the eagle gets his meal there'.

The white-tailed eagle's large size and scavenging habits, combined with its gregarious behaviour and powerful beak and talons, made a potent combination that seems to have caught the eye of humans living in Eurasia throughout history and it seems that it started with the Neanderthals. Talons were used in Native American culture as necklaces but also, in some instances, as medicine[2].

It doesn't surprise me that the most frequent raptor associated with Neanderthals after the golden eagle is the cinereous vulture (Plate 5). It is also known as the Eurasian black vulture. With a 3-metre wing span and a weight that reaches 12.5 kilos, it is one of the largest and heaviest raptors in the world. You easily appreciate its bulk when you first see the bird in flight. It appears like a dark board, its wings being long and broad, that manoeuvres across the sky without having to beat its wings. It is an accomplished glider that regains altitude when it needs by soaring on thermal currents produced by the sun heating the land.

It is equally spectacular on the ground. When at a carcass and other vultures are about it moves forward by jumping, with wings partly opened to enhance the impression of size and head slightly lowered. Two tufts of feathers on each shoulder stick out vertically to complete the image of a giant that all must beware and move out of the way from. Neanderthals would have observed this behaviour at close quarters and admired the king of the vultures. Its mystique may have been enriched by its solitary nature. Unlike the gregarious griffon vultures, cinereous vultures scan the countryside for carcasses on their own. Sometimes a few might gather at a carcass, but driven by hunger not sociality. Unlike the other vultures, which nest on cliff ledges, cinereous vultures nest on tall trees. The practice would have allowed them to spread across large areas of the flat Eurasian Plain where other vultures could not reach.

The other two vultures on the Neanderthals' favourites list are the bearded vulture, or lammergeier, and the griffon vulture. The griffon is the archetypal vulture: big, featherless neck and head, going around in raucous gangs picking carcasses of herbivores clean. The lammergeier is something else (Plate 6). There is nothing else like it in the world. It too is huge but its elongated shape and massive diamond-shaped tail make it a striking creature. It is especially so on the ground.

This bird invented cosmetics. The adults are naturally white but they bathe in iron-rich springs and pools, or even by dust-bathing in sand produced after pecking on red rocks[9]. They then spread the red colour over the feathers. Other researchers ascribe a sanitary function by suggesting that the pigment—ochre—is active in sunlight, producing chemicals that can kill viruses and bacteria and convert smelly organic substances into neutral carbon dioxide gas[10]. The intriguing suggestion has been made that humans started to use ochre for similar sanitary purposes over 100 000 years ago, by observing lammergeiers. If this was indeed the case then the ritual behaviour associated with ochre in humans would have had a biomimetic origin, by observing the behaviour of lammergeiers.

In 2010, archaeologist Joao Zilhao and colleagues[11] published a paper in the *Proceedings of the National Academy of Sciences USA* in which they put forward evidence of what they considered to be symbolic behaviour by Neanderthals. In Neanderthal sites in south-eastern Spain, dated to around 50 000 years ago, they found perforated marine shells alongside lumps of yellow and red pigment. Pigment residues inside another shell were haematite (iron oxide) and pyrite (an iron sulphide). A perforated scallop shell was also found in a site that was 60 kilometres inland. It had been painted on the outside with a mix of haematite and goethite (an iron hydroxide).

These results certainly indicated modern behaviour by the standards set by the archaeologists. Is it a coincidence that the Neanderthals were using at least some of the components that went into lammergeier makeup? Did these pigments offer the Neanderthals advantages that went beyond cosmetics? This may be a stretch of the imagination but it does leave us wondering. Zilhao's sites were in areas that would have been regularly frequented by lammergeiers and we know that Neanderthals caught the big vultures. Was the unique orange coloration of the lammergeiers a source of wonder? Did Neanderthals observe the bathing ritual of the lammergeier? It would have only needed one Neanderthal to observe it and copy what they saw. If adopted, the practice would have spread socially after that.

In the 1950s American archaeologist Ralph Solecki excavated a 13 000-year old hunter-gatherer site at Shanidar in Iraq. He found a mass of animal bones within a deposit of red earth close to a stone structure[12]. All the bones were goat skulls and bird bones. With the exception of a great bustard, the bird bones belonged entirely to lammergeier, griffon vulture, and white-tailed eagle. They were wing bones which had been carefully separated from the rest of the bird, as cut marks revealed, and they were apparently covered in ochre and thought to have been part of a shamanic ritual[3].

In an interpretation of these observations, archaeologist Steven Mithen thought that, while vultures could have become tame around settlements and could have been captured with bait, eagles would have been more challenging[12]. He concluded that the eagles would have had to have been young birds stolen from the nests and then hand-reared, but this would appear to be based on a misunderstanding of the behaviour of white-tailed eagles.

These observations are remarkable but not unique in the Middle East. The 8000-year-old Turkish Neolithic site of Çatalhöyük has produced some of the oldest bird images painted on a prepared surface anywhere in the world[3]. The birds are vultures. Much earlier, around 11 900 years ago at Göbekli Tepe in present-day Turkey, hunter-gatherers were erecting massive pillars. Among the animals depicted in these pillars are vultures[13]. These and other sites in the Middle East are showing a very close, apparently spiritual, connection between the last of the Eurasian hunter-gatherers and vultures.

The 'big six' birds that Neanderthals took for their feathers and talons are birds that would not normally, with one exception, be found in sub-Saharan Africa. The exception is the lammergeier, which has populations that seem to have spread southwards down the Rift Valley all the way to South Africa. There are other vultures in sub-Saharan Africa. Rüppell's, white-backed, and Cape vultures are griffons, but there is no cinereous vulture. The large vulture of sub-Saharan Africa is the lappet-faced vulture. The golden eagle is found in North Africa but does not penetrate the Sahara Desert southwards. It is the Verreaux's (or black) eagle that occupies parts of sub-Saharan Africa where it specializes on hunting rock hyrax. The white-tailed eagle is replaced by the smaller African fish eagle. Neither Verreaux's or African fish eagles scavenge except on very rare occasions. Lanzarote is about as south as ravens get. In Africa there are several other species of raven, all smaller and with comparably limited ranges.

To date, all the evidence of raptor exploitation for feathers and talons comes from Eurasia. We have nothing comparable in Africa. The practice spans a long time, from 130 000 years ago to recent historical times. It transcends the Neanderthal–Modern

Human boundary and it involves a small group of raptors and the raven. With the arrival of humans in North America we find similar practices with the same or very closely related species. We do not know if the practice was independently started in North America or was, instead, carried over by people crossing the Bering Strait from Siberia.

Recent attempts to attribute modern behaviours to Neanderthals were criticized on the grounds that the Neanderthals were simply copying, being acculturated[14] by the newly arrived modern humans. The age of the behaviours we are observing here, the Eurasian and North American connection with the species of birds involved, and the fact that the practice was taking place at least 50 000 years before any Modern Humans reached Eurasia make me raise the alternative question: did Modern Humans learn raptor and corvid catching practices, and subsequent symbolism, from the Neanderthals? We now know that we readily accepted their genes so why not also their customs?

CHAPTER 18

HOW TO SKIN A VULTURE

The Strait of Gibraltar, where I live, is a major migration route for birds travelling between Europe and Africa. These migrations involve many species which cross the Sahara Desert twice each year[1]. A number of these species are raptors and they cross in the thousands. To count 10 000 or more raptors in a day from the top of the Rock of Gibraltar, in the right season and weather conditions, is not unusual.

The reason why so many raptors gather here is to make the short sea-crossing to Africa in the autumn and back in the spring. Some of these large and bulky raptors are simply unable to fly over long stretches of water. Because of their large size they are unable to deposit large amounts of fat prior to migration. Smaller songbirds, many weighing between 10 and 30 grams, do deposit fat before long flights; at those weights even doubling your body weight doesn't affect your flight performance that much. With the larger raptors depositing fat in this way would not just compromise flight performance, it would prevent the birds from taking off in the first place.

Often, I sit on the cliffs of Gibraltar above Gorham's Cave watching the flocks of raptors—the Americans call them kettles—circling above my head and wonder how many times Neanderthals would have done the same. Most of the species which I see passing overhead somehow seem to have managed to find their way into the caves at one time or another. A number may have simply flown in looking for somewhere to rest and never made it out, but, as we have seen already, others were taken by the Neanderthals themselves.

A major consequence of not being able to put down large amounts of fat is that raptors have to find alternative means of migrating over long distances. Because they cannot have large fuel tanks they have gone for efficiency instead. They make the most of their broad wings to soar on thermal currents which are produced as the sun heats up the land. If you are going to watch raptors on migration don't get up too early. Wait until mid-morning and you will then see the spectacle. So what these birds do is gain height on thermals and then glide horizontally, covering ground, until they lose so much height that they have to catch another thermal. This way they can cover great distances without having to flap their wings, which would mean spending energy.

Thermals don't form over the sea, which is why most raptors avoid long sea crossings. The idea is that when they have to cross a narrow stretch of sea, they soar on one side to a great height and then glide to the other side to make the landfall. This is the theory, and what you read in most textbooks. The reality is quite different. Very often I see a large raptor that has taken off from the North African coast. The journey to the other shore is 14 kilometres but winds don't always let the birds get to where they want to go.

The Rock of Gibraltar is at the north-eastern end of the Strait of Gibraltar. It is 21 kilometres from the North African coast. When winds blow from the west, raptors drift eastwards and reach Europe at Gibraltar. It is still a comparatively short sea crossing but the extra 7 kilometres make a difference. I see them losing height as they cross and many end up almost touching the crests of the waves. They are forced to flap the last kilometre or more and they arrive exhausted, panting, and looking for a place to land and rest. This is not the textbook image of raptor migration but it is a real one and one that Neanderthals knew and probably exploited.

The risks of crossing over the sea are so great that quite complicated migration routes have evolved. With the advent of GPS and geolocator tracking we are only now beginning to learn what these birds are prepared to do. Perhaps the most cumbersome of the migrants is the short-toed snake eagle. This species arrives in Europe in February and leaves in September; the migration periods are stretched out because immature birds don't keep to schedule so you can see eagles arriving as late as June.

One recent study[2] tracked a number of juvenile short-toed snake eagles that had been born in southern Italy. You would have been forgiven for having assumed that these birds would have migrated south towards Sicily and, from there, crossed the relatively short sea stretch of 140 kilometres to Tunisia. The tracking results surprised everyone. The birds flew north, coasting the entirety of Italy; they then turned west to pass southern France and then south-west to cross the Pyrenees and the entire length of the Iberian Peninsula to reach Gibraltar. From here they crossed into North Africa. That was the huge pressure exerted by the sea on a species that had invested so heavily on soaring flight.

We are also learning just how hazardous migration is for these birds. The crossing of the Sahara Desert involves getting across the huge ecological barrier as quickly as possible but many, especially juveniles, die in the process. One study[3] showed that juvenile mortality over the Sahara accounted for 50 per cent of all juvenile mortality in the species studied and one in three attempts at crossing ended in death.

Birds also die when crossing over the sea and I see this happening every year. Exhausted raptors coming over the sea try to land on the water. It is a fatal mistake. Others get harassed by local nesting gulls and get driven into the sea. Unless they can be rescued by boat, they also drown. Yet others get attacked by peregrine falcons which nest on the cliffs, as they have been doing since Neanderthal times. Peregrines dig their talons into the heads of the tired raptors, many three times their size. The outcome of these David-and-Goliath contests invariably end in favour of David. One common source of permanent injury or death is loss of vision when a talon has penetrated the eye.

One result of all this macabre business is that I collect quite a few specimens of dead raptors which I put in the freezers of the Gibraltar Museum for future reference. One of the main species that I get, and which gives me great storage nightmares because of its size, is the griffon vulture. These large birds are simply not designed to flap their wings and the crossing of the sea is just too much for some of them.

As we were learning about the way Neanderthals were processing large raptors, seeing the cut marks of their tools on the wing bones of birds such as griffon vultures, we felt that we would learn how they did it if we could replicate the marks. We had plenty of vulture specimens so all we needed were the tools. Fran Giles is an excellent flint knapper who works with me in the museum. I asked him to get some nodules of flint and replicate Neanderthal tools. It is a marvel to watch how he does it and you understand how the process of producing flakes with sharp cutting edges is really something that requires a detailed understanding of how flint fractures, where to strike the blow, and a vision of what you are going to produce after three or four chains of action in the process. It requires not only great skill but also advanced cognition.

One summer, during the one day that we have off each week from excavations, we decided to bring out three griffon vultures from the freezer. We brought them out the day before to allow them to defrost but the July temperatures in Gibraltar ensured that the carcasses were nice and soft when we got ready to perform the operation. We were all there, including Ruth and Jordi, our taphonomists who had done such sterling work on the bird bones. This kind of experimental work is something which they do regularly. It may involve, for example, leaving a carcass out on a mountain and monitoring it over a period of years to see how the bones get dispersed, for example by the action of scavengers. I have seen some impressive footage taken by them of brown bears on a carcass of a deer in northern Spain.

Fran and Jordi got started on the production of the flakes that we would use to cut the vultures open. The image could have been reminiscent of a Neanderthal scene had it not been for the safety goggles which Health and Safety rules prescribed. I don't know what the injury rate was for Neanderthal knappers but I suspect they knew what they were doing. The shaping of the flakes didn't take them too long and we were ready for action. The idea was to cut through the ventral side, the thorax and belly, to then begin to pull the skin away. The vulture was on the ground, dorsal side against the earth, belly up. The flakes were surprisingly sharp, cutting through the skin as easily as a scalpel. That, in itself, was a lesson of how well the cutting edges of the flakes worked in this context.

The important thing to bear in mind at this stage was not to get overexcited with the cutting and puncture the intestine. It would have meant a hasty retreat from the carcass of the vulture. While we were opening up the first of the vultures we debated whether such an animal was edible. Were the birds being caught purely for their feathers? I certainly didn't find it particularly appetizing and I remember another occasion when I cleaned a griffon vulture to obtain its complete skeleton. The process involved some boiling of the flesh to remove it from the bones. The smell stayed in my mind for weeks afterwards during which time I kept well away from having chicken soup.

I have since looked hard for references of humans eating vultures in the ethnographical literature and I have only found one case, the Bandas of Andhra Pradesh in southern India[4]. This is an isolated case involving a small tribe, who reportedly also ate crows and other scavenging birds. It seems that vultures are not a regular feature of our menu anywhere and they probably weren't for the Neanderthals either. They took them for other reasons, as we now know.

The process of skinning the vulture took nearly two hours. I'm sure it didn't take the Neanderthals anywhere near that long. We were learning as we went along. The trick was to pull the skin right down the tarsi to isolate the legs. Then the wings took their time to do. What struck me most was what we found on the wing. Built for efficient flying as we have seen, the wing of the griffon vulture is the epitome of economy: it consists of the wing bones, small muscles and a tendon to hold the wings in position, and the insertion points for the feather quills. You wouldn't get much meat cutting into these areas. Yet it is here, in the wing, that we found most of the cut marks made by the Neanderthal flakes. They were after something other than meat.

With care it was possible to pull the body away from the skin round the wings and back to completely isolate the carcass. With a few direct cuts we were left with a complete cloak of vulture feathers consisting of both wings and the tail. When we looked at the wing bones, there too were the tell-tale marks of our cutting process. With time and practise we became faster at skinning the vultures but I'm sure we never reached the dexterity of the Neanderthal.

All our work had paid dividends. We had separated a small group of raptors and corvids that were special for the Neanderthals. We had understood how they would have captured these birds and that they did so at specific times of the year. They planned their activities and didn't behave like Klein's brown hyenas in South Africa. We knew that the practice had continued for thousands of years across a large geographical area, so it wasn't a one-off either. Our experiments now confirmed that the marks that we had found on the ancient bird bones had been the product of skinning the birds for their feathers. The process had required the skilful manufacture of stone tools that most of us would be unable to make. Having done all this we now had another question that we needed to ask. Were Neanderthals only catching birds for their feathers, or were there species which they took to eat?

CHAPTER 19

PIGEONS AND CHOUGHS

I had been struck by the sheer quantity, not just diversity, of bird bones recovered from Gorham's Cave for some time. The work on the use of raptors and corvid feathers by Neanderthals, important though it had been, had also been a distraction because we had stopped looking at other bird species. This was natural given the importance of what we had been finding with the raptors and corvids but I was keen to return and have another look at other birds. This work continues today so we can expect further results to be published in the future, but for now we can look at two types of bird that were among the most abundant at the site, if numbers of remains are anything to go by. They are pigeons and choughs.

Pigeons are present in almost every Neanderthal occupation level at Gorham's Cave. The majority are rock doves, ancestors of today's feral pigeon. This is what we might expect as these are colonial birds that nest on cliff ledges and hollows. Gibraltar must have been rock dove paradise. It isn't always possible to separate the bones of rock doves from its close relative the stock dove so a proportion of the identified bones were attributed to one or other of these birds. They are very similar except that the stock dove prefers trees to cliffs. A third pigeon—the wood pigeon—is significantly larger and also a bird of trees. It also found its way into Gorham's Cave. It didn't take too long to decide that pigeons would be a good group to start with[1].

At the end of the study 1724 bones of pigeons had been carefully examined under the microscope and they represented a minimum of 198 individual birds. This was a fantastic sample that allowed us to say things about Neanderthals and their exploitation of pigeons with confidence. We found clear cut marks made by Neanderthal stone tools on wing bones but also on leg bones and on the sternum. The proportion of bones with such marks was around 2 per cent. This is actually quite remarkable when you consider that much of the processing of the pigeons would not have required the use of tools. After skinning and removing the feathers from the birds, hands and teeth would have been the best tools for removing meat, fat, and cartilage from the bones.

We could prove that this was the case as we found Neanderthal tooth marks and associated damage in a number of the bones. The imprints and alterations on the bones were the result of disarticulation or even direct consumption by the Neanderthals. We also found that the Neanderthals had been roasting the pigeons in the fire. Over 11 per cent of the bones showed evidence of having been in the fire and over 18 per cent of these showed evidence of double colouring. What is this double colouring and why is it important? The bones that were evenly burnt could have been thrown into the fire after the bird had been eaten, so that our evidence might simply have showed a sanitary practice.

Double colouring resolves this question. It is observed when the entire surface of the bone has not been exposed to the fire with the same intensity. It is what typically happens when parts, or the whole, of the prey are placed on the fire for roasting. The parts of bone that have no meat are exposed to the fire at a higher intensity and the degree of burning in these areas is higher. You can contrast this with areas of bone that are covered by a large mass of muscle. These bones remain unmodified, or slightly modified, by the fire and show different coloration.

It shouldn't surprise us that Neanderthals roasted pigeons. They controlled fire and we have underestimated their abilities. In 2011, Amanda Henry at the Smithsonian and colleagues published results[2] of an examination of the dental calculus of Neanderthals in Spy in Belgium and Shanidar in Iraq. They recovered microscopic plant fossil remains and starch grains from the teeth of the Neanderthals which showed that they had been consuming a wide range of plants, such as date palms, legumes, and grass seeds. What was most important of all was that they found that many of the grass seed starches showed damage of the kind that unequivocally signals cooking.

Returning to Gorham's Cave, were the Neanderthals the main agents bringing the pigeons to the cave? This certainly seems to have been the case. Only 0.81 per cent of the bones showed evidence of having being gnawed by carnivores and 0.22 per cent showed damage due to digestion by birds of prey.

Our sample was a large one so we were confident that the results showed that the Neanderthals had been systematic in their practice, and that the behaviour was not sporadic—the brown hyena syndrome. What's more, we were able to demonstrate that the Neanderthals had been roasting pigeons in at least 11 different archaeological levels and that they had been carrying out the practice from at least 67 000 years ago and that the custom continued for another 40 000 years after that.

A striking aspect that came from this work was the comparison with the Modern Humans who came to Gorham's Cave after the Neanderthals had disappeared. They also caught pigeons and behaved just like the Neanderthals had done. From their actions on pigeon bones at least, Modern Humans were indistinguishable from Neanderthals. It was no surprise to us. We had found, when comparing the exploitation of marine molluscs at Gorham's Cave, that Neanderthals and Modern Humans behaved in a similar fashion and took the same species[3].

When we compare Neanderthal and Modern Human behaviour from a similar time frame in the same locality, what we find is that they are inseparable. Many of the comparisons that have been made in the past have not been from the same place[4]. This means that we cannot distinguish whether the differences that are seen have to do with real differences between Neanderthals and Modern Humans or, instead, with the food resources and habitats available in each place. My suspicion is that most, if not all, of what have been claimed as differences in Neanderthal and Modern Human ecology have been due to place and not the humans themselves.

This suspicion was corroborated by a paper that was published in the journal *Nature* in 2017[5]. Laura Weyrich from the University of Adelaide and a large team of co-workers looked at Neanderthal ancient DNA in the dental plaque of five Neanderthals to look at what they had been eating. They found that at Spy Cave in Belgium the Neanderthal diet was largely meat and included woolly rhinoceros and wild sheep. This contrasted with the Neanderthals at El Sidrón in northern Spain who had been eating mushrooms, pine nuts, and moss. There was no meat at all in the diet of the Neanderthals from El Sidrón.

The other group of birds that we looked at was the choughs. These are corvids and come as two species—red-billed and yellow-billed (or Alpine; Chapter 6). At Gorham's Cave, they were even more frequent and abundant than the raven and they had also been implicated in the Neanderthal feather extraction practice. Although they are very different from other corvids, in anatomy and behaviour, we had suggested that some at least may have been caught by ambush hunting. Choughs occasionally come to carcasses but they are not regulars, like the ravens or the magpies.

It is possible that these cave dwellers were coming down close to the camp sites to take scraps. My twenty-first-century experience of the red-billed choughs is that they are wary creatures. In contrast, I have found the yellow-billed choughs to be very approachable, in winter at least. You can visit the skiing resorts in the Pyrenees, for example, and these choughs are everywhere in the villages. When there is a thick cover of snow you can easily bring them down from the roof tops by enticing them with scraps of bread.

Our pigeon paper was published in 2014. We followed this with another paper two years later[6] in which we compared the pigeons with the choughs. We had 804 remains of these birds and 518 came from Neanderthal contexts, so here we had another large sample to play with. Our larger sample, two years after the first paper, showed Neanderthal intervention on pigeon and corvid bones in 80 per cent of the archaeological levels that we examined; over 13 per cent of the bones examined showed evidence of human-caused damage. As before, we found no differences between Neanderthals and Modern Humans.

We found that the pigeon pattern repeated itself with the choughs: cut marks, burning, and over-extension of the elbow. The action of the Neanderthals was not concentrated solely on the wing bones, as was the case with raptors and the raven, but also on leg bones. This indicated that choughs were being caught for food as well as for their feathers. Size may have something to do with this.

The raven weighs between 1 and 1.5 kilos. It is a very large bird that matches some of the medium-sized raptors. The red-billed chough, on the other hand, weighs between 275 and 375 grams and the yellow-billed chough 170–250 grams. They are significantly smaller than the raven. The rock dove is in the 200–350 gram range, comparable with the choughs. Finally, the larger wood pigeon reaches half a kilo. The difference between the pigeons, the choughs, and the raven is that the latter is solitary and the former are sociable, colonial, and can form large flocks of hundreds of birds. From an economic standpoint, large numbers of medium-sized choughs and pigeons make sense. They also produce many young, particularly the pigeons. Gorham's Cave and its surrounding rock faces were ideal habitat for pigeons and choughs. For the Neanderthals living alongside them, these birds offered them a guaranteed and sustainable food supply. There are other animals too that would fit this profile—partridges and rabbits in particular—and we are looking at these as I write these lines in Gibraltar.

We have come a long way in our understanding of the Neanderthal diet. They certainly killed and ate large mammalian herbivores but we must wonder how frequent such kills were and how dependent they were on this food source. We have seen how there were clear regional differences in diet. Neanderthal diet ranged from strict meat-eaters to vegetarians with all omnivorous options open to them in between. They cooked their food. In places, like Gibraltar, they exploited the great variety of food resources that were available to them. We find many seeds of stone pine in their camp fires so it is very likely that here, like elsewhere, they ate plants and their products. They also consumed marine molluscs, seals and dolphins (Chapter 13), herbivorous mammals, tortoises, and birds. That is a broad spectrum of food resources.

We also know now that the exploitation of foods that have been considered difficult to catch, such as birds, was not beyond them. The catching of birds can no longer be considered a sporadic practice. The results from Gorham's Cave show us that these were regular practices that had long traditions that spanned tens of millennia. They had been in use long before any Modern Humans had reached Europe. They would have clearly needed substantial planning to execute efficiently and, importantly, a clear knowledge of where and when, as the winter exploitation of raptors shows. They must have had technology to accompany the bird-catching practices but we have seen how difficult it is to find perishables in the archaeological record.

One line of research that may advance us significantly on the question of perishables is the analysis of residues left on the stone tools used by the Neanderthals. In 2013 Bruce Hardy and colleagues[7] published some very interesting results of such an analysis of Neanderthal stone tools from Abri du Maras in France, dating to around 90 000 years ago. They were able to show that Neanderthals exploited a wide range of resources at this site including large mammals, fish, ducks, raptors, rabbits, mushrooms, plants, and wood. They found twisted fibres on stone tools, which they saw as evidence of making string or cordage. These Neanderthals, the authors suggested, might have even had complex projectile technology, something that only Modern Humans were meant to have had. Put together with what we have seen so far, this really changes our view of Neanderthals, or it should.

It is now time to turn our attention to one of the great blunders that has halted progress in our understanding of human behaviour, Neanderthals included. That is the idea that we can somehow subdivide the natural world, from a human hunter-gatherer perspective, into two types of prey—fast- and slow-moving.

CHAPTER 20

FEEDING THE VULTURES

Birds, hares, and rabbits, it has been said, are fast-moving prey, difficult to catch. This idea is so absolutely wrong that it defies belief how it could ever have taken root as the support for one of the major hypotheses of Neanderthal and Modern Human hunting behaviour of the last three decades. I think that the answer lies in the fact that there has been very little input of natural history in the development of these hypotheses. To understand Neanderthal hunting, it's simply not enough to be a specialist of Neanderthal anatomy; nor of the anatomy of the animals that lived alongside the Neanderthals; nor of the taphonomic processes that can give us clues of who processed the bones and the shells and how they did it; nor of the stone tools that were made and how they were made. Most important of all, we need to understand the behaviour and ecology of the potential prey species. We might be able to read accounts in textbooks about the behaviour of this or that species but, in isolation, we will never gain an understanding.

So let's put things right. Let's start with the hares and the rabbits. We cannot talk of the two animals as if all the species can be clustered into this simple definition. The Order Lagomorpha is composed of two families: the Ochotonidae (the pikas) and the Leporidae (hares and rabbits). If we take a look at the three main continental landmasses relevant to us here, we find that Africa has 12 species of hares and rabbits. Eurasia (excluding south and south-east Asia) has 15 and North America 23 species. Eurasia also has 24 species of pika and North America has two.

The problem is that even the 'standard' hare and rabbit don't behave in a similar manner. Hares tend to be fast-running, open habitat species that often rely on camouflage to remain undetected by predators. Hares 'freeze' when threatened. There have been occasions when I have found myself standing right beside a hare. The animal has relied on its camouflage and stayed put. Had I wanted to I could have caught the animal with my hands. So much for fast-moving prey. Had a Neanderthal been in my situation, and they would have been in those situations a lot more than me, they would have caught the hare and left no trace of the capture method in the archaeological record.

Rabbits are more colonial and sociable than hares and tend to feed close to their burrows. They run fast in short bursts that get them back to the safety of their tunnels. Traditional techniques for catching rabbits have relied on blocking up the exits of the burrows except one which will become the only escape route. A net would be placed on this exit but it is not necessary. An alert person can catch a rabbit as it emerges with their hands too. The way to encourage them to come out is usually by smoking them out, although in historical times predators such as ferrets have been used to drive panic inside the burrows. Had a Neanderthal caught a rabbit using any of these methods, no trace of the capture method would have been left for archaeologists to find.

If lumping all rabbits and hares into a single category is unwise, imagine doing the same for the 10 000 species of birds in the world, ranging from ostriches and emus to the tiniest hummingbirds. I have already given some examples of how close I have been able to get to birds. In Chapter 9 I showed how we got to within touching distance of a variety of seabirds in their breeding colonies on the North Sea. Catching them would not have required technology, just bare hands, and although we needed a boat to get to the islands in the twenty-first century there would have been many mainland colonies of seabirds at the time of the Neanderthals that would not have required boats. Gibraltar was one such site. In Chapter 10 I advanced some ideas of how cryptic ground birds might have been caught by Neanderthals. It would make sense to include the hare in here as a cryptic species that stays put when it detects a predator. The ways of catching these animals involve careful stalking and a keen eye, having if you like a specific search image of the prey. Technology, like small nets on a pole, might help in these cases.

What I want to describe now are ways of getting close to large and powerful birds. I am going to give two personal experiences with wild griffon vultures in the Pyrenees. On both occasions my son Stewart was with me and we were able to document the experiences with photographs.

The first was at a site in the Catalan Pyrenees near an abandoned village called Buseu. We had arranged an expedition with our guide Jordi (not the zooarchaeologist referred to previously), a cheerful Catalan, who met us at an agreed time and place the evening before. We followed him up a mountain, first on a narrow road, which predictably gave way to a track which went on for miles. After an hour or so we arrived in Buseu. It was an eerie experience, to see all the houses shut. The steeple of the church stood above the other buildings. Nobody had lived here for years and Jordi had bought the village. He was fixing some of the buildings in his spare time and had repaired and converted one of them into a splendid chalet where his visitors could stay.

That evening we were treated to a sumptuous meal after having watched the sun go down over the distant peaks of the Pyrenees. There was a chill in the mountain air. We went to bed early with the usual excitement of what would happen the following morning. After an early breakfast Jordi and his son abruptly developed an urgency. We had to go and we did. I have learnt in these situations never to question the ways of mountain people. They know what is needed and it's best not to ask. The first instruction was to get our kit into his 4×4. Once we were in we started climbing up a steep rocky slope. I'm glad my own vehicle wasn't required. Stewart and I are used to off-roading but this ascent, with a back tray loaded with carrion, required prior knowledge.

As he drove, Jordi gave us instructions. He was going to briefly pause at a particular point where Stewart and I would alight and enter a hide which would be situated to our left. We were to go in quickly and silently. He would pick us up at sunset. As we drove up the steep slope we could see several dozen griffon vultures flying low over us. The sun had barely risen but these birds must have been sleeping nearby and were using the updraughts from the slopes in place of the thermals that would form in due course. All the same it was surprising for us to see so many vultures circling above our heads so early in the morning.

Jordi stopped the car and we got out in accordance with his instructions. He and his son drove on. We got into the hide and quickly brought our equipment out so as not to miss any of the action. When we had the cameras and lenses mounted on the tripods we sat down and looked out. We couldn't believe the scene in front of us.

The car had stopped in a glade among the mountain conifers. Jordi and his son were outside in full view of the vultures. They started to bring the carrion out and scatter it on the ground. The griffons started to land about 100 metres from them. At first ten, then twenty; five minutes later we had 300 griffons on the ground. They were not the only ones. There were lammergeiers and Egyptian vultures in the air but a couple of cinereous vultures had also landed. We had all the four species of European vultures together right in front of us.

The griffons plucked up courage and advanced towards the food. It was a tidal wave of griffons, edging each time closer to the meat, and to Jordi and his son who were still there. Soon they were a few metres away and started the typical feeding frenzy. It was each vulture for himself or herself and they lost all perception of the humans who were by then right beside them. Had he wanted to, Jordi could have caught any number of vultures there and then. Instead he left in his vehicle, parting the vultures aside like a modern-day Moses, down the slope and we were left on our own.

In time all four species of vulture came down and delighted us with their antics. As food ran out we observed another vulturine habit that was familiar to us from other sites we had visited. Instead of flying away, they rested. First upright, but eventually lying flat on their bellies. They could barely keep their eyes open after such a full meal. I could understand exactly. It was siesta time for the vultures.

Some vultures gorge themselves to such a degree that they have to do this, allow time for digestion before being able to take off. Had we come out at that point we could have rushed these birds and caught one or two. I'm not speculating here. In Spain in the past, people have caught vultures in this way although I'm not sure what for, as they were never eaten.

A knock on the door of the hide signalled Jordi's arrival and he had a surprise. No vehicle. We had to walk with our heavy gear all the way down to the chalet. As we walked he explained that his vehicle had not broken down. This was what he always did. Whenever he took the vehicle up it carried food and the vultures had learnt to recognize the signal. If he drove without food, to pick us up, the vultures would be confused. This is why so many vultures were flying low over our heads first thing that morning. They had recognized Jordi's 4×4.

The second experience was even more startling. We had heard that there was a man somewhere in the Pyrenees who fed wild vultures from his hand. We just had to see this, so we found him through a convoluted route involving several contacts and contacts of contacts. We stayed overnight in a country house close to where we were to meet, according to our instructions. The meeting place was the village of Santa Cilia de Panzano. Never trust your vehicle's GPS. We could never have imagined that there would be two Santa Cilias but there were and we went to the wrong one. It cost us over an hour but when we finally got to the right place our guide, Manu (the man who fed the vultures), seemed happy enough to see us. We wasted no further time and drove up another Pyrenean track, this time in the central region in the province of Huesca. We stopped our cars in a widening of the track and started to get our equipment out. Manu produced a wheelbarrow from his car and put it to one side as if it was the most normal thing to do. He briefed us. We were to follow him single file, make no noise, and do as he instructed. It was the way of mountain people who feed vultures, after all.

Manu brought out several bags of meat and one with chickens' eggs. Apparently, he explained, the Egyptian vultures loved to eat eggs; the other vultures too but especially the Egyptians. I remembered as a child seeing the photographs of the recently discovered behaviour of Egyptian vultures using rocks as tools to break ostrich eggs in Africa and my mind raced with ideas of possible experiments which we could do and which Manu confirmed he had done. Yes, he had given the European vultures ostrich eggs here and they broke them with rocks. They must have picked up the idea in their African winter quarters.

We started to walk along a narrow path on the side of a slope. Manu had put on a bright pink windcheater. He told us as we went on that he always wore it when going to feed the vultures. It was his signal to them and they recognized it. We didn't realize just how well they would recognize it. Soon vultures were flying low over our heads but then, as if not caring to wait for Manu's ritual, they started to land on the path ahead of us and on the rocks beside us, barely a metre away. Manu was shooing them off with his hands but they kept coming back. We had never seen anything like this or been so close to wild vultures, except when rescuing them from the sea at Gibraltar.

We arrived at the feeding place, an open rocky slope. Manu told us where to sit and left the empty wheelbarrow with us. He sat down some 10 metres away and was rapidly engulfed by a mass of griffon vultures. At first he threw morsels a short distance away and the vultures scrambled noisily to get there first. After a while Manu had had enough throwing and simply held a piece of meat in his glove-protected hand. Three vultures lunged forward and one got the piece. Yes, here we had wild vultures taking food from a man's hand (Figure 12).

Stewart was positioned closest to the birds and was photographing them with a wide-angle lens. He was lying flat on the ground (Plate 7). At one point Manu threw a morsel in Stewart's direction and the vultures came crashing in, without caring that

Figure 12 Manu feeding wild griffon vultures.

Stewart was there, and one thumped right into him. Stewart had got very close indeed to these difficult-to-catch, fast-flying creatures. Perhaps I should say that they got close to him.

Manu claimed to recognize individual birds which he talked to by name. It was an unforgettable experience. He had started feeding vultures as a young man thirty years before and continued the practice several times a week right to today. It was a testimony to his persistence that he had achieved the confidence of so many wild animals. Thinking Neanderthals on the way back home, Stewart and I were buzzing with the experience we had just had. We had finally put the fast-flying, difficult-to-catch idea to bed.

CHAPTER 21

THE HASHTAG AND THE END OF THE LONG ROAD TO NEANDERTHAL EMANCIPATION

It was the summer of 2012. We had picked ourselves up from missing out on the raptor feather exploitation premiere, and had our own paper in the pipeline for imminent publication. We were in the middle of our annual excavations at Gorham's and Vanguard Caves (Plate 8). I remember the moment clearly. I was in Gorham's Cave, near the outer section, when I was asked to go to the inner part of the cave, where Paco wanted to see me.

Paco Giles is one of the best field archaeologists I have ever met, and it has been a privilege to work with him for three decades. Paco has the rare mix of archaeological knowledge and experience of the natural world. He is a naturalist. When Paco calls you have to respond immediately so I went up towards his position to find him crouched, with his head torch on and looking intently down at the ground. I asked him what it was that he wanted to see me about and he pointed at the ground. At first I couldn't see anything, and then he pointed out to me some lines which seemed to form a criss-cross pattern.

We stared at the lines. And we stared further. What could they be and who had made them? The problem that was in the back of our minds, even though we hadn't really spoken to each other, was that we were looking at a level that had been occupied by Neanderthals. It was a level which we had excavated and, in the process, uncovered the lines. They had been covered by 60 centimetres of sediment which only contained Neanderthal artefacts. The implication was that the lines had been made by a Neanderthal.

We didn't want to believe this. It would be a huge claim and we would have to have clear proof before we said anything, so we embarked on an exercise of scepticism. We threw every possibility at it that would show that it had not been done by the Neanderthals. We brought in our own specialists, particularly our geomorphologist Joaquin Rodriguez Vidal from the University of Huelva. Joaquin's knowledge of geomorphology and geological processes is always a source of comfort and confidence for me when interpreting what is happening in our caves. This one was going to test him to the limit.

Time passed and Joaquin produced a detailed analysis of how the various microscopic layers covering the lines had formed, apparently a process that started after the lines had been sealed by deposit. He was able to tell the story in intimate detail. The lines were grooves that had been made in the ground. They made up what seemed to be an engraving.

It was now the summer of 2013. A year had passed and we were confident that what we had was an engraving made by a Neanderthal (Figure 13). We didn't know what it meant, and we still don't today, but this was something unique, something nobody had found before. We had managed to keep the secret between a handful of trustworthy colleagues but we felt it was time to publish. Before going down this path, and bearing in mind the importance of the claim, I felt that we needed a second

Figure 13 The Hashtag.

opinion. The others agreed. The choice of who to confide in was clear. It had to be Francesco d'Errico who was, for us, the world's leading expert on ancient markings on bones and rocks. This was going to be a first even for him.

So one July day in 2013 I picked up the phone thinking that everyone, like me, spent the summer in the field, working. Francesco works in the University of Bordeaux but the call reached him in his native Italy where he was on holiday. He explained that he was in Liguria with his family and that it would be impossible for him to get away. He would let me know when he could come. A week later he was in Gibraltar.

We took Francesco down to the cave. We had previously briefed him and now it was time to show him. He sat where Paco had sat a year earlier. He stared at the engraving. He changed position and the angle of the light and he stared further. I was desperate to know what he thought but didn't want to rush him. I also feared the worst—that he would not agree with our interpretation. Then, he suddenly turned and started to say something like 'OK, we're going to need this bit of equipment, and also this and that'. I cannot remember the exact words but at that point I couldn't contain myself anymore and asked 'Well, is it?' to which Francesco replied, with a grin, 'Of course it is!'

We embarked on a detailed study of the engraving, which was to take us another year. We couldn't take the engraving to the lab and to have attempted to make a cast would have compromised the physical and chemical integrity of the grooves themselves. So a special microscope was brought down to the cave. We carried out experiments to understand how the engraving had been made. By then we had accurate measurements of each and every groove so we tried to replicate the engraving. To do this we took a piece of rock of the same kind as that in which the lines were engraved. We started to replicate the grooves with replica Neanderthal tools made of the same material as those used by them in Gibraltar.

Francesco started and my daughter-in-law, Jade, offered to be his note taker. He pushed into the rock and drew the first line. There was a pause as the width and depth of the groove was measured. He struggled to make the second impression as he found it difficult to keep to the line. This was harder than it seemed. Eventually, after sixty repeated strokes we reached the dimensions of the original groove, having lost the point of one of the tools, which snapped off in the experiment. In the end the entire engraving was completed and we calculated that it would have taken two hours to make. This was clearly not a doodle. Somebody with considerable skill had made it.

We then thought of discarding options which critics would raise. We quickly discarded natural lines formed by water action. There were such lines in the cave but they were of completely different characteristics and dimensions. Another criticism would be that they were butchery marks, of the tools slipping while cutting meat. So off went Jade to the butcher and came back with a chunk of pork with the skin still on. Francesco tried but couldn't control the lines which were all over the place. There was no way that the marks were butchery marks. We were there. We could show in fine detail that we had found an engraving made by a Neanderthal.

Two years after the discovery, after a great deal of discussion and experimentation, and with a splendid team who kept the secret for this long, the paper was published in *Proceedings of the National Academy of Sciences USA*[1]. We didn't claim the engraving to be art. Many others have done so since. For us, we were happy to show that a Neanderthal had made some lines deliberately and that the lines had no functional purpose. The person who made the engraving must have done others before, as it required skill and experience. What it meant we didn't know, but it showed that someone, some 40 000 years ago, had made an abstract pattern[2]. It showed, above all else, that the person had cognitive skills comparable to that of a Modern Human. That Neanderthal was in every way human.

We have come a long way in recent years and the Neanderthal behavioural evidence has made the idea of a Modern Human Cognitive Revolution[3], either at 50 000 years ago or indeed at any other stage, completely untenable. Most recently, two papers have been published that seem to support further the idea that Neanderthals were artists and jewellers, and that they may have been painting cave walls as far back as 64 800 years ago[4].

Even though it is strongly supportive of the views that I have put forward, we need to treat this latest claim with some caution as it is largely based on the age of the paintings, from a time when Modern Humans had not reached Europe. Until we find clear palaeontological or archaeological signs implicating the Neanderthals directly, the door must remain ajar. Recent genetic discoveries of anatomically unknown human lineages[5] and 'ghost' species[6] are telling us that we can no longer assume the occupiers of sites purely from the age of deposits.

Genetics has completely revolutionized in no time at all the entire story of human origins. We now know that those people of non-African descent carry Neanderthal genes today and the whole process of human evolution resembles the pattern of a braided stream[7], with lineages separating and sometimes coalescing once again in time. Linear ancestor-descendant schemes and even branching trees no longer represent our evolution satisfactorily.

This is not a pattern that supports the notion of a 'Tree of Knowledge' mutation that suddenly appeared in us literally overnight some 50 000 years ago[3]. It is a pattern that, instead, shows the great degree of equality that existed among different human lineages. In some cases, as we have seen, the Neanderthals kept Modern Humans away from Europe. That's hardly a marker of Modern Human superiority. Instead, it has been chance that has had a major role to play in our existence and the extinction of the Neanderthals[8].

What seems to have happened is that Modern Humans slowly penetrated Neanderthal territory and there was significant interbreeding between populations. That entry seems to have been made easier by receding Neanderthal populations caused by loss of their favourite woodland habitats across central Eurasia[9]. In the past, followers of the Replacement Model[10] even interpreted evidence of apparently symbolic behaviour by Neanderthals to have been the outcome of the inferior Neanderthals having had to learn how to make beads and similar objects from the superior Modern Humans. Ironically, it now seems that such practices as the catching of large eagles and wearing their feathers for symbolic purposes were probably picked up by Modern Humans watching and learning it from the Neanderthals.

Related to brain function, the size of the neocortex has been linked with the ability of different primates to operate successfully in groups of particular sizes[11]. The idea was that as the neocortex got bigger in the course of evolution, so bearers of larger neocortexes could engage in social relations within increasingly larger groups. The notion that humans could ideally handle relations with around 150 people is based on this Social Brain Hypothesis. It has been used to propose that abilities resulting from a mutation that occurred 50 000 years ago, allowing us to interact with even more people than 150, triggered the Cognitive Revolution[3]. The problem is that there is no genetic evidence of such a mutation, nor archaeological evidence for a revolution 50 000 years ago, and now even the Social Brain Hypothesis is being called into question[12].

It is now abundantly clear that the list of component parts of the Cognitive Revolution, as listed initially by Mellars, did not appear all at once, but gradually over a long period. It is also evident that most of those elements were also a part of the Neanderthal makeup: they made blades; they made complex tools; they had personal ornaments in the form of eagle feathers; they used ochre either to paint themselves or to make paintings, or both; they made engravings in cave walls; and they had sophisticated economic and social organization that included detailed planning of hunting activities at specific times of the year for particular prey. The prey often included birds, those apparently fast-flying animals that were impossible to catch.

We have a lot more to learn about the Neanderthals but we know enough already to be able to say that they were our cognitive equals and that they were not replaced by cognitively superior humans. I cannot help feeling that the way that we have seen the silent Neanderthals[13] is practically the same way that we viewed other humans when we discovered them in new worlds[14]. In a recent interview for a documentary I was asked if I would like to meet, if it were ever possible, a living Neanderthal. My initial reaction was to say that I would but I paused and hesitated. I replied that I would not. If the history of how we had dealt with other humans when we first met them, and of our subsequent treatment of them, was anything to go by, then it would be best for the Neanderthals not to be discovered living on this planet today.

If there is an exception to the rule, it is provided by those early Modern Humans and Neanderthals who first met tens of thousands of years ago. Because, based precisely on our recent history, we didn't think it possible that we could have ever met other humans and not wiped them out, we came up with the simplistic Replacement Model.

In his book *Sapiens*, Yuval Harari[15] has put forward the idea that fictions accumulate immense power and imagined realities exert force in the world. This may well be the case. Ironically, one of the best examples has been the story that we have told about our own rise at the expense of inferior humans. It has been as influential as the best creation myths. Alas, it was wrong. Instead, we are now seeing how complex and beautiful the story of all humans who live and have lived on this planet really is. It is time to wipe out, once and for all, the residual notion that we can classify humans by levels of cognition. It is time to welcome the Neanderthals into our global community.

BIRD SPECIES CITED IN THE TEXT

Vernacular Name	Scientific Name
Brent goose	*Branta bernicla*
Barnacle goose	*Branta leucopsis*
Greylag goose	*Anser anser*
Gadwall	*Anas strepera*
Mallard	*Anas platyrhynchos*
Pintail	*Anas acuta*
Garganey	*Anas querquedula*
Teal	*Anas crecca*
Marbled teal	*Marmaronetta angustirostris*
Red-crested pochard	*Netta rufina*
Pochard	*Aythya ferina*
Tufted duck	*Aythya fuligula*
Steller's eider	*Polysticta stelleri*
King eider	*Somateria spectabilis*
Velvet scoter	*Melanitta fusca*
Common scoter	*Melanitta nigra*
Long-tailed duck	*Clangula hyemalis*
Red-legged partridge	*Alectoris rufa*
Quail	*Coturnix coturnix*
Red-throated diver	*Gavia stellata*
Storm petrel	*Hydrobates pelagicus*
Northern fulmar	*Fulmarus glacialis*
Cory's shearwater	*Calonectris borealis*

APPENDIX 1: BIRD SPECIES CITED IN THE TEXT

Vernacular Name	Scientific Name
Manx shearwater	*Puffinus puffinus*
Balearic shearwater	*Puffinus mauretanicus*
White stork	*Ciconia ciconia*
Glossy ibis	*Plegadis falcinellus*
Purple heron	*Ardea purpurea*
Northern gannet	*Morus bassanus*
Shag	*Phalacrocorax aristotelis*
Great cormorant	*Phalacrocorax carbo*
Osprey	*Pandion haliaetus*
Bearded vulture	*Gypaetus barbatus*
Egyptian vulture	*Neophron percnopterus*
Griffon vulture	*Gyps fulvus*
Cinereous vulture	*Aegypius monachus*
Short-toed snake eagle	*Circaetus gallicus*
Booted eagle	*Hieraaetus pennatus*
Spanish imperial eagle	*Aquila adalberti*
Golden eagle	*Aquila chrysaetos*
Verreaux's eagle	*Aquila verreauxii*
Bonelli's eagle	*Aquila fasciata*
Red kite	*Milvus milvus*
Black kite	*Milvus migrans*
African fish eagle	*Haliaeetus vocifer*
White-tailed eagle	*Haliaeetus albicilla*
Bald eagle	*Haliaeetus leucocephalus*
Rough-legged buzzard	*Buteo lagopus*
Common buzzard	*Buteo buteo*
Great bustard	*Otis tarda*
Kori bustard	*Ardeotis kori*
Little bustard	*Tetrax tetrax*
Water rail	*Rallus aquaticus*

APPENDIX 1: BIRD SPECIES CITED IN THE TEXT

Vernacular Name	Scientific Name
Spotted crake	*Porzana porzana*
Coot	*Fulica atra*
Eurasian stone curlew	*Burhinus oedicnemus*
Bush stone curlew	*Burhinus grallarius*
Black-winged stilt	*Himantopus himantopus*
Lapwing	*Vanellus vanellus*
Woodcock	*Scolopax rusticola*
Snipe	*Gallinago gallinago*
Collared pratincole	*Glareola pratincola*
Kittiwake	*Rissa tridactyla*
Great black-backed gull	*Larus marinus*
Herring gull	*Larus argentatus*
Yellow-legged gull	*Larus michahellis*
Arctic tern	*Sterna paradisaea*
Black tern	*Chlidonias niger*
Great skua	*Stercorarius skua*
Little auk	*Alle alle*
Guillemot	*Uria aalge*
Razorbill	*Alca torda*
Great auk	*Pinguinus impennis*
Atlantic puffin	*Fratercula arctica*
Wood pigeon	*Columba palumbus*
Turtle dove	*Streptopelia turtur*
Scops owl	*Otus scops*
Snowy owl	*Bubo scandiacus*
Eagle owl	*Bubo bubo*
Tawny owl	*Strix aluco*
Red-necked nightjar	*Caprimulgus ruficollis*
European nightjar	*Caprimulgus europaeus*
Square-tailed nightjar	*Caprimulgus fossii*

Vernacular Name	Scientific Name
Common swift	*Apus apus*
Pallid swift	*Apus pallidus*
Roller	*Coracias garrulus*
Hoopoe	*Upupa epops*
Great spotted woodpecker	*Dendrocopos major*
Iberian green woodpecker	*Picus sharpei*
Lesser kestrel	*Falco naumanni*
Kestrel	*Falco tinnunculus*
Eleonora's falcon	*Falco eleonorae*
Hobby	*Falco subbuteo*
Peregrine falcon	*Falco peregrinus*
Southern grey shrike	*Lanius meridionalis*
Siberian jay	*Perisoreus infaustus*
Iberian azure-winged magpie	*Cyanopica cooki*
Magpie	*Pica pica*
Red-billed chough	*Pyrrhocorax pyrrhocorax*
Yellow-billed chough	*Pyrrhocorax graculus*
Jackdaw	*Coloeus monedula*
Carrion crow	*Corvus corone*
Raven	*Corvus corax*
Willow tit	*Poecile montana*
Siberian tit	*Poecile cincta*
Great tit	*Parus major*
Woodlark	*Lullula arborea*
Skylark	*Alauda arvensis*
Crested lark	*Galerida cristata*
Calandra lark	*Melanocorypha calandra*
Sardinian warbler	*Sylvia melanocephala*
Short-toed treecreeper	*Certhia brachydactyla*
Spotless starling	*Sturnus unicolor*

APPENDIX 1: BIRD SPECIES CITED IN THE TEXT

Vernacular Name	Scientific Name
Blackbird	*Turdus merula*
Mistle thrush	*Turdus viscivorus*
Robin	*Erithacus rubecula*
Pied flycatcher	*Ficedula hypoleuca*
Black redstart	*Phoenicurus ochruros*
Northern wheatear	*Oenanthe oenanthe*
Black-eared wheatear	*Oenanthe hispanica*
House sparrow	*Passer domesticus*
Spanish sparrow	*Passer hispaniolensis*
Tree sparrow	*Passer montanus*
Rock sparrow	*Petronia petronia*
Dunnock	*Prunella modularis*
Yellow wagtail	*Motacilla flava*
White wagtail	*Motacilla alba*
Tawny pipit	*Anthus campestris*
Meadow pipit	*Anthus pratensis*
Water pipit	*Anthus spinoletta*
Chaffinch	*Fringilla coelebs*
Hawfinch	*Coccothraustes coccothraustes*
Pine grosbeak	*Pinicola enucleator*
Greenfinch	*Chloris chloris*
Goldfinch	*Carduelis carduelis*
Corn bunting	*Emberiza calandra*

MAMMAL SPECIES CITED
IN THE TEXT

Vernacular Name	Scientific Name
Woolly mammoth	*Mammuthus primigenius*
Wild cat	*Felis sylvestris*
Lynx	*Lynx lynx*
Spanish lynx	*Lynx pardina*
Lion	*Panthera leo*
Leopard	*Panthera pardus*
Spotted hyena	*Crocuta crocuta*
Brown hyena	*Hyaena brunnea*
Wolf	*Canis lupus*
Arctic fox	*Vulpes lagopus*
Red fox	*Vulpes vulpes*
Brown bear	*Ursus arctos*
Cave bear	*Ursus spelaeus*
Atlantic grey seal	*Halichoerus grypus*
Mediterranean monk seal	*Monachus monachus*
Wolverine	*Gulo gulo*
Badger	*Meles meles*
Weasel	*Mustela nivalis*
Polecat	*Mustela putorius*
Horse	*Equus caballus*
Woolly rhinoceros	*Coelodonta antiquitatis*
Wild boar	*Sus scrofa*
Moose	*Alces alces*

Vernacular Name	Scientific Name
Reindeer	*Rangifer tarandus*
Red deer	*Cervus elaphus*
Giant deer	*Megaloceros giganteus*
Aurochs	*Bos primigenius*
Barbary sheep	*Ammotragus lervia*
Ibex	*Capra ibex*
Spanish ibex	*Capra pyrenaica*
Musk ox	*Ovibos moschatus*
Chamois	*Rupicapra rupicapra*

ENDNOTES

Chapter 1 Nana and Flint

1. You can see examples of Kennis & Kennis' wonderful work on their web page http://kenniskennis.com/site/Home/
2. The German specimen was found in the Feldhofer Cave in the Neander Valley near Dusseldorf in Germany in 1856. It was initially thought to have been a pathological modern human (I. Tattersall & J. Schwartz (2000), *Extinct Humans*, Westview Press, New York). The Gibraltar specimen had been found in 1848 in Forbes' Quarry and presented to the Gibraltar Scientific Society by Captain Edmund Flint (C. Stringer (2000), 'Gibraltar and the Neanderthals 1848–1998', in C. B. Stringer, R. N. E. Barton, & J. C. Finlayson (eds), *Neanderthals on the Edge*, Oxbow Books, Oxford. pp 133–8). It was the German specimen that was given the scientific name *Homo neanderthalensis* by William King in 1864 (M. H. Day (1986), *Guide to Fossil Man*, Fourth Edition, Cassell, London).
3. Dorothy Garrod was a distinguished Cambridge archaeologist. Her work in Gibraltar, between November 1925 and December 1926, was the turning point in her career. Here she found the skull of a Neanderthal child whom she called Abel. This Abel is Flint in this book. In 1939 she was appointed Disney Professor at Cambridge but could not take up her appointment after the end of the Second World War as women did not exist in the University's Statutes, effectively making her an 'invisible' Professor (W. Davies & R. Charles (eds) (1999), *Dorothy Garrod and the Progress of the Palaeolithic. Studies in the Prehistoric Archaeology of the Near East and Europe*, Oxbow Books, Oxford).
4. Marcellin Boule of the Museum of Natural History in Paris reconstructed the near-complete Neanderthal skeleton from La Chapelle-aux-Saints that had been found in 1908. Between 1911 and 1913 Boule published his results, creating the racist image of a primitive, ape-like caveman that came to dominate our view of the Neanderthal (C. Stringer & C. Gamble (1993), *In Search of the Neanderthals: Solving the Puzzle of Human Origins*, Thames & Hudson, London).

5. According to Polish sociologist and philosopher Zygmunt Bauman, 'In dichotomies crucial for the practice and the vision of social order the differentiating power hides as a rule behind one of the members of the opposition. The second member is but *the other* of the first, the opposite (degraded, suppressed, exiled) side of the first and its creation. Thus abnormality is the other of the norm, deviation the other of law-abiding, illness the other of health, barbarity the other of civilization, animal the other of human, woman the other of man, stranger the other of the native, enemy the other of friend, 'them' the other of 'us', insanity the other of reason, foreigner the other of the state subject, lay public the other of the expert. Both sides depend on each other, but the dependence is not symmetrical. The second side depends on the first for its contrived and enforced isolation. The first depends on the second for its self-assertion.' (Z. Bauman (1991), *Modernity and Ambivalence*, Polity Press, Cambridge).

6. P. Mellars & C. Stringer (1989), 'Introduction', in P. Mellars & C. Stringer (eds), *The Human Revolution: Behavioural and Biological Perspectives on the Origins of Modern Humans*, Edinburgh University Press, Edinburgh, pp 1–14.

7. A. Nowell (2010), 'Defining Behavioral Modernity in the Context of Neandertal and Anatomically Modern Human Populations', *Annual Review of Anthropology* 39: 437–52.

8. S. McBrearty & A. Brooks (2000), 'The revolution that wasn't: a new interpretation of the origin of modern human behavior', *Journal of Human Evolution* 39: 453–563.

9. L. M. Hurcombe (2014), *Perishable Material Culture in Prehistory: Investigating the Missing Majority*, Routledge, London.

10. P. Mellars (1991), 'Cognitive Changes and the Emergence of Modern Humans in Europe', *Cambridge Archaeological Journal* 1: 63–76.

11. A blade is essentially a flake twice as long as it is wide, although some archaeologists refine the definition further. Archaeologists Ofer Bar-Yosef at Harvard and Steve Kuhn at the University of Arizona reviewed the evidence and concluded that blades appeared thousands of years before the Upper Palaeolithic (equated to Modern Humans) and that there was no justification in linking blades per se to any aspect of hominid anatomy or to any major change in the behavioural capacities of hominids. Importantly, they added that evidence from other regions of the world demonstrated that evolutionary trends in Pleistocene Eurasia were historically contingent and not universal (O. Bar-Yosef & S. Kuhn (1999), 'The Big Deal about Blades: Laminar Technologies and Human Evolution', *American Anthropologist* 101: 322–38.

12. The appearance of tools made of bone, antler, and ivory coincides with the occupation of the Eurasian Steppe by Modern Humans. This was a treeless landscape and the use of alternative materials to wood can be seen as an adaptation to local conditions and not as an example of modern behaviour. It seems clear that certain technological elements, if not all, had a clear ecological significance and depended on availability of raw materials. There was great flexibility in the use of particular tool kits, both by Neanderthals and Modern Humans (C. Finlayson (2004), *Neanderthals and Modern Humans: An Ecological and Evolutionary Perspective*, Cambridge University Press, Cambridge).

13. The earliest naturalistic art in Europe is from Chauvet Cave in France and is dated to around 32 000 years ago (J. Clottes (2003), *Chauvet Cave: The Art of Earliest Times*, University of Utah Press, Salt Lake City). A recently discovered hand stencil dated at 39 900 years ago and a painting of a babirusa ('pig-deer') dated to 35 400 years ago in Sulawesi, Southeast Asia, raise questions regarding the origins and age of naturalistic art (M. Aubert et al. (2014), 'Pleistocene Cave Art from Sulawesi, Indonesia', *Nature* 514: 223–8). To these we can add further finds, reported in 2017, of symbolic activity in Wallacea, South-east Asia, dated between 30 000 and 22 000 years ago, consisting of personal ornamentation and portable art, alongside evidence of pigment processing and use in deposits of the same age dated rock art in the surrounding region (A. Brumm (2017), 'Early human symbolic behaviour in the Late Pleistocene of Wallacea', *Proceedings of the National Academy of Sciences USA* 114: 4105–10).

14. C. Renfrew (2007), *Prehistory: Making of the Human Mind*, Weidenfeld & Nicolson, London.

15. The Neolithic, associated with the first farmers, is thought to have started in the Middle East around 10 000 years ago (O. Aurenche et al. (2011), 'Proto-Neolithic and Neolithic Cultures in the Middle East—the Birth of Agriculture, Livestock Raising, and Ceramics: A Calibrated 14C Chronology 12 500–5 500 cal BC', *Radiocarbon* 43: 1191–202).

16. P. Mellars (2007), 'Rethinking the Human Revolution: Eurasian and African Perspectives', in P. Mellars, K. Boyle, O. Bar-Yosef, & C. Stringer (eds), *Rethinking the human revolution*, McDonald Institute Monographs, Cambridge, pp 1–11.

17. S. McBrearty (2007), 'Down with the Revolution', in P. Mellars, K. Boyle, O. Bar-Yosef, & C. Stringer (eds), *Rethinking the human revolution*, McDonald Institute Monographs, Cambridge, pp 133–51.

18. J. J. Hublin et al. (2017), 'New fossils from Jebel Irhoud, Morocco and the pan-African origin of *Homo sapiens*', *Nature* 546: 289–95.

Chapter 2 Neanderthals and Birds

1. M. C. Stiner et al. (1999), 'Paleolithic Population Growth Pulses Evidenced by Small Animal Exploitation', *Science* 283: 190–4; M. C. Stiner, N. D. Munro, & T. A. Surovell (2000), 'The Tortoise and the Hare', *Current Anthropology* 41: 39–73; M. C. Stiner (2001), 'Thirty Years on the "Broad Spectrum Revolution" and paleolithic demography', *Proceedings of the National Academy of Sciences USA* 13: 6993–6; M. C. Stiner & N. D. Munro (2002), 'Approaches to Prehistoric Diet Breadth, Demography and Prey Ranking Systems in Time and Space', *Journal of Archaeological Method and Theory* 9: 181–214.
2. Archaeologists have used a different terminology for the African Palaeolithic compared to that of Eurasia, which is confusing. In Eurasia, the Middle Palaeolithic represents the Neanderthals and other 'archaic' humans and the Upper Palaeolithic represents Modern Humans. In Africa, the Middle Stone Age (MSA) represents Archaic Modern Humans and the Late Stone Age (LSA) represents Behaviourally Modern Humans. The African and Eurasian terminologies are roughly equivalent but are not the same. There is still a lot of uncertainty regarding the timing of transitions from one age to another.
3. T. E. Steele & R. G. Klein (2009), 'Late Pleistocene Subsistence Strategies and Resource Intensification in Africa', in J. J. Hublin & M. P. Richards (eds), *The Evolution of Hominin Diets. Integrating Approaches to the Study of Palaeolithic Subsistence*, Springer, Dordrecht, pp 113–26.
4. R. G. Klein (2000), 'Archaeology and the Evolution of Human Behavior', *Evolutionary Anthropology* 9: 17–36.
5. C. Finlayson (2009), *The Humans Who Went Extinct: Why Neanderthals died out and we survived*, Oxford University Press, Oxford.
6. R.G. Klein (1995), 'Anatomy, Behavior, and Modern Human Origins', *Journal of World Prehistory* 9: 167–98.
7. J. J. Shea (2017), *Stone Tools in Human Evolution. Behavioral Differences among Technological Primates*, Cambridge University Press, Cambridge.
8. K. E. Westaway (2017), 'An early modern human presence in Sumatra, 73,000–63,000 years ago', *Nature* 548: 322–8.
9. C. Clarkson et al. (2017), 'Human occupation of northern Australia by 65,000 years ago', *Nature* 547: 306–13.
10. W. Liu et al. (2015), 'The earliest unequivocally modern humans in southern China', *Nature* 526: 696–700.
11. H. S. Groucutt et al. (2018), '*Homo sapiens* in Arabia by 85,000 years ago', *Nature Ecology and Evolution* https://doi.org/10.1038/s41559-018-0518-2

12. T. Higham et al. (2011), 'The earliest evidence for anatomically modern humans in northwestern Europe', *Nature* 479: 521–4.

13. C. Finlayson (2014), *The Improbable Primate: How Water Shaped Human Evolution*, Oxford University Press, Oxford.

14. K. Prufer et al. (2017), 'A high-coverage Neandertal genome from Vindija Cave in Croatia', *Science* 10.1126/science.aao1887.

15. B. Vernot & J. M. Akey (2017), 'Resurrecting Surviving Neandertal Lineages from Modern Human Genomes', *Science* 343: 1017–21.

16. R. E. Green et al. (2010), 'A Draft Sequence of the Neandertal Genome', *Science* 328: 710–22.

17. P. Rincon (2010), *Neanderthal genes 'survive in us'*, BBC News Online http://news.bbc.co.uk/2/hi/sci/tech/8660940.stm

18. M. Kuhlwilm et al. (2016), 'Early gene flow from early modern humans into Eastern Neanderthals', *Nature* 530: 429–35.

19. S. Sankararaman et al. (2012), 'The Date of Interbreeding between Neandertals and Modern Humans', *PLoS Genetics* 8: e1002947.

20. M. D. Gregory et al. (2017), 'Neanderthal-derived genetic variation shapes modern human cranium and brain', *Scientific Reports* doi 10.1038/s41598-017-06587-0

Chapter 3 Lessons from the Arctic

1. The name given to the coniferous belt that stretches across Boreal regions of Eurasia.

2. The period popularly equated to the Ice Ages, from approximately 2.5 million years ago to 10 000 years ago.

3. For example woolly mammoth *Mammuthus primigenius* and woolly rhinoceros *Coelodonta antiquitatis*.

4. T. Birkhead (1993), *Great Auk Islands: A field biologist in the Arctic*, T & A D Poyser, London.

5. Bird species' scientific names are in Appendix 1.

6. E. de Juana & E. Garcia (2015), *The Birds of the Iberian Peninsula*, Christopher Helm, London.

7. Archaeological contexts are distinct levels within a site that reflect separate episodes, for example different moments of occupation of the site. They could be events separated by thousands of years or within shorter time spans, even within a human generation.

8. M. Shrubb (2013), *Feasting, Fowling and Feathers: A History of the Exploitation of Wild Birds*, T & A D Poyser, London.

9. This was the number of species identified at the time of our visit. The number has since risen to 160 species.

Chapter 4 The Long-tailed Duck

1. S. Cramp (ed) (1977), *Handbook of the Birds of Europe, the Middle East and North Africa: The Birds of the Western Palearctic*, Volume 1, Oxford University Press, Oxford.
2. C. Finlayson (2009), *The Humans Who Went Extinct: Why Neanderthals died out and we survived*, Oxford University Press, Oxford.
3. S. E. Churchill (2014), *Thin on the Ground: Neandertal Biology, Archeology, and Ecology*, Wiley Blackwell, Ames.
4. C. Finlayson (2004), *Neanderthals and Modern Humans: An Ecological and Evolutionary Perspective*, Cambridge University Press, Cambridge.
5. I used my data from Finlayson (2004) in combination with that published in T. H. van Andel & W. Davies (eds) (2004), *Neanderthals and modern humans in the European landscape during the last glaciation*, McDonald Institute Monographs, Cambridge.
6. Mammal species' scientific names are in Appendix 2.
7. B. Kurtén (1968), *Pleistocene Mammals of Europe*, Aldine, New Brunswick.
8. V. Geist (1998), *Deer of the World: Their Evolution, Behavior, and Ecology*, Stackpole Books, Mechanicsburg.
9. Wild olive *Olea europaea* and stone pine *Pinus pinea*.
10. J. S. Carrión et al. (2008), 'A coastal reservoir of biodiversity for Upper Pleistocene human populations: palaeoecological investigations in Gorham's Cave (Gibraltar) in the context of the Iberian Peninsula', *Quaternary Science Reviews* 27: 2118–35.
11. Among the birds found alongside long-tailed duck at Gibraltar are typical summer migrants from Africa: lesser kestrel, collared pratincole, red-necked nightjar, and pallid/common swifts.
12. Santa Catalina in Biscay.
13. These tablelands can exceed altitudes of 1000 metres.

Chapter 5 The White Ghost

1. E. Potapov & R. Sale (2012), *The Snowy Owl*, T & A D Poyser, London.
2. https://www.news4jax.com/news/local/snowy-owl-makes-rare-appearance-in-florida

Chapter 6 Gibraltar

1. C. Finlayson et al. (2006), 'Late Survival of Neanderthals at the southern-most extreme of Europe', *Nature* 443: 850–3; C. B. Stringer, R. N. E. Barton, & J. C. Finlayson (eds) (2000), *Neanderthals on the Edge*, Oxbow Books, Oxford.
2. N. Emery (2003), 'Are Corvids "Feathered Apes"? Cognitive Evolution in Crows, Jays, Rooks and Jackdaws', in S. Watanabe (ed), *Comparative Analysis of Mind*, Keio University, Tokyo, pp 181–214.
3. It has recently been estimated that there has been a 75 per cent decline in total insect biomass in protected areas in Europe in the last 27 years (C. A. Hallmann et al. (2017), 'More than 75 per cent decline over 27 years in total flying insect biomass in protected areas', *PLoS One* https://doi.org/10.1371/journal.pone.0185809
4. Birds that occupy intertidal mudflats and estuaries where they feed by wading and probing in the mud with their long bills.
5. A number of indeterminate *Aquila* eagle remains in the caves are almost certainly of this species.
6. J. Rodriguez-Vidal et al. (2013), 'Undrowning a Lost World—The Marine Isotope Stage 3 Landscape of Gibraltar', *Geomorphology* 203: 105–14.
7. G. Finlayson (2006), *Climate, Vegetation and Biodiversity—A Multiscale Study of the South of the Iberian Peninsula*, PhD Thesis, Anglia Ruskin University, Cambridge.

Chapter 7 The Dynamic World of Dunes

1. At Lago Grande di Monticchio in Italy, forest and wooded steppe replaced steppe and vice versa rapidly during the last glacial cycle (120 000–10 000 years ago), on average every 142 years (J. R. M. Allen et al. (1999), 'Rapid environmental changes in southern Europe during the last glacial period', *Nature* 400: 740–3.
2. F. d'Errico et al. (1998), 'Neanderthal Acculturation in Western Europe?: A Critical Review of the Evidence and its Interpretation', *Current Anthropology* 39: S1–S44.
3. The species that would have been year-round residents and have been found in the caves are cinereous vulture, common buzzard, kestrel, red-legged partridge, quail, wood pigeon, tawny owl, hoopoe, Iberian green woodpecker, great spotted woodpecker, woodlark, Sardinian warbler, blackbird, mistle thrush, southern grey shrike, great tit, short-toed tree creeper, Iberian azure-winged magpie, magpie, jackdaw, spotless starling,

rock sparrow, chaffinch, hawfinch, goldfinch, greenfinch, and a sparrow species (probably Spanish sparrow or tree sparrow). These would have been joined in the spring by migrants from Africa: white stork, black kite, booted eagle, hobby, turtle dove, scops owl, red-necked nightjar, and pied flycatcher, the last species probably only on passage and not remaining to breed. Others would have arrived from the north to spend the winter like they do today: red kite, woodcock, dunnock, robin, and black redstart.

Chapter 8 Lakes and Plains

1. As a result of global warming at the end of the last Ice Age.
2. Flysch.
3. Red-crested pochard, marbled teal, mallard, a small duck (either teal or garganey), a larger duck (either gadwall or pintail), pochard, tufted duck, long-tailed duck, common scoter, velvet scoter, and a species of eider (*Somateria*).
4. Purple heron, glossy ibis, water rail, spotted crake, coot, collared pratincole, black-winged stilt, lapwing, and black tern.
5. Roller, calandra lark, crested lark, short-toed larks (*Calandrella*), skylark, white wagtail, yellow wagtail, meadow pipit, tawny pipit, water pipit, northern wheatear, black-eared wheatear, and corn bunting.

Chapter 9 The Great Auk

1. T. Birkhead (1993), *Great Auk Islands: A field biologist in the Arctic*, T & A D Poyser, London.
2. F. d'Errico (1994), 'Birds of the Grotte Cosquer: The Great Auk and Palaeolithic Prehistory', *Antiquity* 68: 39–47.
3. Northern fulmar, Manx shearwater, great cormorant, shag, Atlantic puffin, razorbill, guillemot, little auk, kittiwake, and great black-backed and herring gulls.

Chapter 10 Big Eyes

1. E. Pearce, C. Stringer & R. I. M. Dunbar (2013), 'New insights into differences in brain organization between Neanderthals and anatomically modern humans', *Proceedings of the Royal Society B* 280: 20130168.
2. http://www.bbc.com/news/science-environment-21759233
3. S. Traynor et al. (2015), Brief Communication: 'Assessing Eye Orbits as Predictors of Neanderthal Group Size', *American Journal of Physical Anthropology* 157: 680–3. The Social Brain Hypothesis has also recently

come under fire: L. E. Powell et al. (2017), 'Re-evaluating the link between brain size and behavioural ecology in primates', *Proceedings of the Royal Society B* doi 10.1098/rspb.2017.1765.

4. C. Finlayson (2014), *The Improbable Primate: How Water Shaped Human Evolution*, Oxford University Press, Oxford.

5. M. Shrubb (2013), *Feasting, Fowling and Feathers: A History of the Exploitation of Wild Birds*, T & A D Poyser, London.

6. R. E. Moreau (1951), 'The British Status of the Quail and Some Problems of its Biology', *British Birds* XLIV: 257–76.

Chapter 11 Digging in the Cave

1. The four caves are Gorham's, Vanguard, Ibex, and Devil's Tower. They are all situated on the eastern flank of the Rock of Gibraltar, facing the Mediterranean Sea.

2. Bergmann's Rule. An ecogeographical rule which states that within a species, those populations living further north will have larger body sizes than those further south. The result of increasing body size is a lowering of the surface:volume ratio. As less surface area is exposed to the outside world, relative to size, less heat will be lost from the skin's surface.

3. The radiocarbon method of dating can be used on fragments of charcoal and, in some cases, bone. It gives reliable dates back to around 40 000 years ago after which time the method becomes unreliable.

4. A suite of dating methods is available including optically stimulated luminescence, uranium–thorium, electron spin resonance, and amino acid racemization: C. Renfrew & P. Bahn (2011), *Archaeology: Theories Methods and Practice*, Thames & Hudson, London.

5. Most amphibians, such as frogs or newts, and reptiles have very specific temperature and humidity tolerances. Finding a particular species within a cave deposit indicates that climatic conditions suitable for that species were present when the deposit was formed. If several species with similar requirements are found together, it gives a good indication of climatic conditions at the time.

Chapter 12 Neanderthal Real Estate

1. P. Mellars (1996), *The Neanderthal Legacy: An Archaeological Perspective from Western Europe*, Princeton University Press, Princeton. The specialization of hunting was further emphasized by Mellars: 'Neanderthal groups practised a relatively broad-spectrum foraging pattern, usually involving

substantial exploitation of at least three or four different species—reindeer, horse, large bovids (either *Bos* or *Bison*), and red deer. By contrast, most of the faunas recovered from early Aurignacian [presumed to be Modern Humans, my insert] levels in the same region show a striking specialization on reindeer, with reindeer often comprising more than 90% of the documented remains.' (P. Mellars (1998), 'The Impact of Climate Changes on the Demography of Late Neandertal and Early Anatomically Modern Populations in Europe', in T. Akazawa, K. Aochi, & O. Bar-Yosef (eds), *Neandertals and Modern Humans in Western Asia*, Plenum Press, New York. pp 493–508.) For a contrasting view see D. K. Grayson & F. Delpech (2002), 'Specialized Early Upper Palaeolithic Hunters in Southwestern France?', *Journal of Archaeological Science* 29: 1439–49.

2. C. Finlayson (2004), *Neanderthals and Modern Humans: An Ecological and Evolutionary Perspective*, Cambridge University Press, Cambridge.

3. C. Finlayson et al. (2016), 'Using birds as indicators of Neanderthal environmental quality: Gibraltar and Zafarraya compared', *Quaternary International* 421: 32–45.

4. C. Shipton et al. (2013), 'Variation in Lithic Technological Strategies among the Neanderthals in Gibraltar', *PLoS One* https://doi.org/10.1371/journal.pone.0065185

5. J. Féblot-Augustins (1999), 'Raw material transport patterns and settlement systems in the European Lower and Middle Palaeolithic: continuity, change and variability', in W. Roebroeks & C. Gamble (eds), *The Middle Palaeolithic Occupation of Europe*, University of Leiden, Leiden, pp 193–214.

Chapter 13 Of Seals and Limpets

1. C. W. Marean et al. (2007), 'Early human use of marine resources and pigment in South Africa during the Middle Pleistocene', *Nature* 449: 905–9.

2. R. C. Walter (2000), 'Early human occupation of the Red Sea coast of Eritrea during the last interglacial', *Nature* 405: 65–9.

3. J. J. Hublin et al. (2017), 'New fossils from Jebel Irhoud, Morocco and the pan-African origin of *Homo sapiens*', *Nature* 546: 289–95.

4. M. Cortes-Sanchez et al. (2011), 'Earliest Known Use of Marine Resources by Neanderthals', *PLoS One* 6: e24026.

5. R. G. Klein & K. Cruz-Uribe (1991), 'Exploitation of large bovids and seals at Middle and Later Stone Age Sites in South Africa', *Journal of Human Evolution* 31: 315–34.

6. C. B. Stringer et al. (2008), 'Neanderthal exploitation of marine mammals in Gibraltar', *Proceedings of the National Academy of Sciences USA* 105: 14319–24.

7. R. G. Klein & T. E. Steele (2008), 'Gibraltar data are too sparse to inform on Neanderthal exploitation of coastal resources', *Proceedings of the National Academy of Sciences USA* 105: E115. doi: 10.1073/pnas.0809985106

Chapter 14 Birds of a Feather

1. R. Blasco & J. Fernández Peris (2009), 'Middle Pleistocene Bird Consumption at Level XI of Bolomor Cave (Valencia, Spain)', *Journal of Archaeological Science* 36: 2213–23.
2. The bird family Corvidae, comprising crows, magpies, and related species.
3. M. Peresani et al. (2011), 'Late Neandertals and the intentional removal of feathers as evidenced from bird bone taphonomy at Fumane Cave 44 ky B.P., Italy', *Proceedings of the National Academy of Sciences USA* 108: 3888–93.
4. C. Finlayson et al. (2012), 'Birds of a Feather: Neanderthal Exploitation of Raptors and Corvids', *PLoS One* 7(9): e45927. https://doi.org/10.1371/journal.pone.0045927
5. When the wing bones are held with both hands and stretched to disarticulate them.
6. E. Morin & V. Laroulandie (2012), 'Presumed Symbolic Use of Raptors by Neanderthals', *PLoS One* 7: e32856.
7. H. L. Dibble et al. (2009), 'A Preliminary Report on Pech de l'Azé IV, Layer 8 (Middle Palaeolithic, France)', *PalaeoAnthropology* 2009: 182–219.
8. V. Laroulandie et al. (2016), 'Who brought the bird remains to the Middle Palaeolithic site of Les Fieux (Southwestern France)? Direct evidence of a complex taphonomic story', *Quaternary International* 421: 116–23.
9. D. Radovcic et al. (2015), 'Evidence for Neandertal Jewelry: Modified White-tailed Eagle Claws at Krapina', *PLoS One* 10(3): e0119802. https://doi.org/10.1371/journal.pone.0119802
10. A. Majkic et al. (2017), 'A decorated raven bone from the Zaskalnaya VI (Kolosovskaya) Neanderthal site, Crimea', *PLoS One* 12(3): e0173435. https://doi.org/10.1371/journal.pone.0173435

Chapter 15 The Golden Eagle

1. S. Cramp (ed) (1980), *Handbook of the Birds of Europe, the Middle East and North Africa. The Birds of the Western Palearctic*, Volume 2, Oxford University Press, Oxford.
2. M. Cocker (2013), *Birds and People*, Jonathan Cape, London; P. Mohan (2015), *Hunting with Eagles: In the Realm of the Mongolian Kazakhs*, Merrell, London.

3. S. J. Bodio (2003), *Eagle Dreams: Searching for Legends in Wild Mongolia*, Skyhorse Publishing, New York.
4. G. L. Wilson (1928), *Hidatsa Eagle Trapping*, American Museum of Natural History, New York.
5. Spanish imperial eagles emit a cry that is reminiscent of the bark of a dog.
6. S. E. Churchill (2014), *Thin on the Ground: Neandertal Biology, Archeology, and Ecology*, Wiley Blackwell, Ames.

Chapter 16 Ambushing the Scavengers

1. Coprolites are fossilized dung. In the case of hyenas, that eat large quantities of bone, the coprolites are rich in calcium which gives them solidity and a white coloration.
2. S. Finlayson & C. Finlayson (2016), 'The Birdmen of the Pleistocene: On the relationship between Neanderthals and scavenging birds', *Quaternary International* 421: 78–84.

Chapter 17 The Big Six

1. D. Ratcliffe (1997), *The Raven: A Natural History in Britain and Ireland*, T & A D Poyser, London.
2. T. E. Mails (1972), *The Mystic Warriors of the Plains: The culture, arts, crafts and religion of the Plains Indians*, Doubleday and Company, New York.
3. M. Cocker (2013), *Birds and People*, Jonathan Cape, London.
4. R. Bosworth Smith (1905), *Bird Life and Bird Lore*, John Murray, London.
5. I. L. Baxter (1993 for 1992), 'Eagles in Anglo-Saxon and Norse poems', *Circaea* 10: 78–81.
6. J. del Hoyo, A. Elliott, & J. Sargatal (eds) (1994), *Handbook of the Birds of the World*, Volume 2, Lynx Edicions, Barcelona.
7. D. A. Bannerman (1956), *The Birds of the British Isles*, Volume 5, Oliver & Boyd, Edinburgh.
8. A compound expression with metaphorical meaning, used in Old Norse and Old English poetry.
9. S. Xirouchakis (1998), 'Dust bathing in the Bearded Vulture (*Gypaetus barbatus*)', *Journal of Raptor Research* 32: 322; J. J. Negro (1999), 'The function of the cosmetic coloration of bearded vultures: when art imitates life', *Animal Behaviour* 58: F14–F17; J. J. Negro & A. Margalida (2000), 'How Bearded Vultures (*Gypaetus barbatus*) acquire their orange coloration:

a comment on Xirouchakis (1998)', *Journal of Raptor Research* 34: 62–3; J. J. Negro et al. (2002), 'Iron oxides in the plumage of bearded vultures. Medicine or cosmetics?', *Animal Behaviour* 64: F5–F7.

10. H. Tributsch (2016), 'Ochre Bathing of the Bearded Vulture: A Bio-Mimetic Model for Early Humans towards Smell Prevention and Health', *Animals* 6: doi 10.3390/ani6010007

11. J. Zilhao et al. (2010), 'Symbolic use of marine shells and mineral pigments by Iberian Neandertals', *Proceedings of the National Academy of Sciences USA* 107: 1023–8.

12. S. Mithen (2003), *After the Ice: A Global Human History 20,000–5,000 BC*, Weidenfeld & Nicolson, London.

13. K. Schmidt (2010), 'Göbekli Tepe—the Stone Age Sanctuaries. New results of ongoing excavations with a special focus on sculptures and high reliefs', *Documenta Prehistorica* XXXVII: 239–56.

14. P. Mellars (1999), 'The Neanderthal problem continued', *Current Anthropology* 40: 341–64.

Chapter 18 How to Skin a Vulture

1. R. E. Moreau (1972), *The Palaearctic-African Bird Migration Systems*, Academic Press, London.

2. U. Mellone et al. (2016), 'Individual variation in orientation promotes a 3000-km latitudinal change in wintering grounds in a long-distance migratory raptor', *Ibis* 10.1111/ibi.12401.

3. R. Strandberg et al. (2010), 'How hazardous is the Sahara Desert crossing for migratory birds? Indications from satellite tracking of raptors', *Biology Letters* 6: 297–300.

4. K. M. Rao (1997), 'The Bandas and their Impact on the Population of Vultures in Guntur and Prakasam Districts', *Blackbuck* VIII: 60–3.

Chapter 19 Pigeons and Choughs

1. R. Blasco et al. (2014), 'The earliest pigeon fanciers', *Scientific Reports* 4: 5971.

2. A. G. Henry, A. S. Brooks, & D. R. Piperno (2011), 'Microfossils in the calculus demonstrates consumption of plants and cooked foods in Neandertal diets (Shanidar III, Iraq; Spy I & II, Belgium)', *Proceedings of the National Academy of Sciences USA* 108: 486–91.

3. K. Brown et al. (2011), 'Small Game and Marine Resource Exploitation by Neanderthals: the Evidence from Gibraltar', in N. F. Bicho, J. A. Haws, &

L. G. Davis (eds), *Trekking the Shore: Changing Coastlines and the Antiquity of Coastal Settlement*, Springer, New York, pp 247–72.

4. M. C. Stiner et al. (1999), 'Paleolithic Population Growth Pulses Evidenced by Small Animal Exploitation', *Science* 283: 190–4.

5. L. S. Weyrich et al. (2017), 'Neanderthal behaviour, diet, and disease inferred from ancient DNA in dental calculus', *Nature* 544: 357–62.

6. R. Blasco et al. (2016), 'Pigeons and choughs, a usual resource for the Neanderthals in Gibraltar', *Quaternary International* 421: 62–77.

7. B. L. Hardy et al. (2013), 'Impossible Neanderthals? Making string, throwing projectiles and catching small game during Marine Isotope Stage 4 (Abri du Maras, France)', *Quaternary Science Reviews* 82: 23–40.

Chapter 21 The Hashtag and the End of the Long Road to Neanderthal Emancipation

1. J. Rodríguez Vidal et al. (2014), 'A rock engraving made by Neanderthals in Gibraltar', *Proceedings of the National Academy of Sciences USA* 111: 13301–6.

2. It has become popularly known as the Neanderthal Hashtag because of its resemblance to a # as frequently used, for example, on Twitter.

3. The idea of a Modern Human Cognitive Revolution around 50 000 years ago has been recently revived by Y. N. Harari (2011) in his book *Sapiens: A Brief History of Humankind*, Vintage Books, London. It develops the arguments that had been put forward previously by Paul Mellars and Richard Klein in particular: P. Mellars (1991), 'Cognitive Changes and the Emergence of Modern Humans in Europe', *Cambridge Archaeological Journal* 1: 63–76; P. Mellars (2007), 'Rethinking the Human Revolution: Eurasian and African Perspectives', in P. Mellars, K. Boyle, O. Bar-Yosef, & C. Stringer (eds), *Rethinking the human revolution*, McDonald Institute Monographs, Cambridge, pp 1–11; R. G. Klein (2000), 'Archaeology and the Evolution of Human Behavior', *Evolutionary Anthropology* 9: 17–36.

4. D. L. Hoffman et al. (2018), 'U-Th dating of carbonate crusts reveals Neanderthal origin of Iberian cave art', *Science* 359: 912–15; D. L. Hoffman et al. (2018), 'Symbolic use of marine shells and mineral pigments by Iberian Neandertals 115 000 years ago', *Science Advances* 4: eaar5255.

5. The discovery of the Denisovans is based on genetic material recovered from an undiagnostic bone. To date we do not know what the Denisovans looked like nor indeed the extent of their geographical spread or the time span of their existence; J. Krause et al. (2010), 'The complete mitochondrial DNA genome of an unknown hominin from southern Siberia', *Nature* 464: 894–7.

6. Scientists studying the genetic variation of the *MUC7* gene discovered that an unknown African human population had contributed to the variation of this gene; D. Xu et al. (2017), 'African Hominin Introgression in Africa Contributes to Functional Salivary *MUC7* Genetic Variation', *Molecular Biology and Evolution* 34: 2704–15.

7. C. Finlayson (2013), 'Viewpoint: Human Evolution, from tree to braid', BBC News Online, Science and Environment http://www.bbc.com/news/science-environment-25559172

8. C. Finlayson (2009), *The Humans Who Went Extinct: Why Neanderthals died out and we survived*, Oxford University Press, Oxford.

9. The principal cause of the reduction of the central Eurasian woodland was increasing cold and aridity in the long period leading to the height of the last Ice Age; C. Finlayson & J. S. Carrión (2007), 'Rapid ecological turnover and its impact on Neanderthal and other human populations', *Trends in Ecology and Evolution* 22: 213–22.

10. In his recent interpretation of the Replacement Model, Harari revisits the idea of a replacement of all archaic humans (Neanderthals included) by superior Modern Humans. Among the possible factors which he quotes for the success are better technology and superior social skills, although he does not discard that the process may have even taken the form of genocide; Y. N. Harari (2011), *Sapiens: A Brief History of Humankind*, Vintage Books, London.

11. R. I. M. Dunbar (1998), 'The Social Brain Hypothesis', *Evolutionary Anthropology* 6: 178–90.

12. L. E. Powell et al. (2017), 'Re-evaluating the link between brain size and behavioural ecology in primates', *Proceedings of the Royal Society B* doi 10.1098/rspb.2017.1765

13. 'Silent' not because they couldn't speak, which we know that they could, but because they are not here to defend themselves.

14. D. Abulafia (2008), *The Discovery of Mankind: Atlantic Encounters in the Age of Columbus*, Yale University Press, New Haven.

15. Y. N. Harari (2011), *Sapiens: A Brief History of Humankind*, Vintage Books, London.

FIGURE CREDITS

PLATE CREDITS

INDEX